Also of Interest

China's Economic Development: Growth and Structural Change, Chu-yuan Cheng

Economic Reform in the PRC: In Which China's Economists Make Known What Went Wrong, Why, and What Should be Done About it, edited by George C. Wang

China Briefing, 1981, edited by Robert B. Oxnam and Richard C. Bush

The Chinese Agricultural Economy, edited by Randolph Barker and Radha P. Sinha, with Beth Rose

Food for One Billion: China's Agriculture Since 1949, Robert C. Hsu

China: A Political History, 1917-1980, Fully Revised and Updated Edition, Richard C. Thornton

China Among the Nations of the Pacific, edited by Harrison Brown

China in World Affairs: The Foreign Policy of the PRC Since 1970, Golam W. Choudhury

Technology, Politics, and Society in China, Rudi Volti

Red Guard Factionalism and the Cultural Revolution in Guangzhou (Canton), Stanley Rosen

China's Four Modernizations: The New Technological Revolution, edited by Richard Baum

The People's Republic of China: A Handbook, edited by Harold C. Hinton

Urban Development in Modern China, edited by Laurence J. C. Ma and Edward W. Hanten

The Chinese Ministry of Foreign Affairs, 1968-1980: Revolutionary Politics Versus Continuity, Daniel Tretiak

China Geographer: No. 11: Agriculture, edited by Clifton W. Pannell and Christopher Salter

*Available in hardcover and paperback.

Current Economic Problems in China

Westview Special Studies on China and East Asia

Current Economic Problems in China
Xue Muqiao
edited, translated, and with an
Introduction by K. K. Fung

An analysis of the PRC's current economic problems and a critical
evaluation of the nation's efforts to solve them, this book brings
together papers and speeches by Xue Muqiao, one of China's most prom-
inent economists and one of its key spokesmen for liberal economic
reform. Xue addresses such issues as commune and brigade enterprises;
employment and wages; price adjustments; proportional imbalances among
industries, within industries, and between capital accumulation and
consumption; problems associated with current economic reforms; and
proposals for future reforms. The introduction by K. K. Fung traces
the development of Xue's views since the publication of his earlier
works and evaluates the implications of China's liberal economic
policies for Third World countries, which have long regarded China's
pre-reform economic development as a model to be emulated.

Xue's personal involvement with the major organs of central planning in the PRC makes him uniquely qualified to write a book of this
nature. He served as secretary general of the Committee for Financial
and Economic Affairs of the State Council, vice-chairman of the State
Planning Commission, and director of both the State Statistical
Bureau and the National Price Commission. Currently, he is advisor to
the State Planning Commission as well as director of the Institute of
Economics under the Commission.

Dr. K. K. Fung, translator and editor of the collection, is asso-
ciate professor of economics at Memphis State University. He has had
extensive experience in translating Chinese economic literature into
English; among his translations are *Chinese Economic Planning* (1978)
and *Fundamentals of Political Economy* (1977).

To My Mother,
with love and gratitude
—K.K.F.

Current Economic Problems in China

Xue Muqiao

edited, translated, and with an
Introduction by K. K. Fung

Westview Press / Boulder, Colorado

Westview Special Studies on China and East Asia

Copyright © 1982 by Westview Press, Inc.

Published in 1982 in the United States of America by
     Westview Press, Inc.
     5500 Central Avenue
     Boulder, Colorado 80301
     Frederick A. Praeger, President and Publisher

Library of Congress Catalog Card Number: 82-050237
ISBN 0-86531-404-7

Composition for this book was provided by the editor.
Printed and bound in the United States of America.

Contents

viii

Editor's Introduction

I. CURRENT ECONOMIC PROBLEMS IN CHINA - GENERAL CONTENT

A refreshingly open analysis of China's current economic problems and a critical evaluation of current efforts to solve them, Current Economic Problems in China was written by Xue Muqiao, director of the Institute of Economics under the State Planning Commission of the People's Republic of China.

Current Economic Problems was first published in China by the People's Publishing Company in Beijing in October 1980. The Chinese edition contained 17 papers, reports, and speeches written and delivered mostly in 1979 and 1980. As was typical of a collection of this nature, there was content duplication from one paper to another. To avoid excessive duplication, only 11 papers were selected for this English edition. And in some papers, only parts were translated.

Current Economic Problems deals with: (1) proportional imbalances among industries, within industries, and between capital accumulation and consumption, (2) commune and brigade enterprises, (3) labor employment and wages, (4) price reform, (5) problems encountered in current economic reforms, and (6) proposals for future reforms.

II. XUE MUQIAO - A BIOGRAPHICAL NOTE

Xue's personal involvement with the major organs of central planning in China uniquely qualifies him to write a book of this nature. He served as secretary general of the Committee for Financial and Economic Affairs of the State Council, vice chairman of the State Planning Commission, director of the State Statistical Bureau, and director of the National Price Commission. Currently, he is adviser to the State Planning Commission as well as director of the Institute of Economics under the Commission.[1]

Xue is one of the most, if not the most, read economists in China and overseas today. His earlier book,
China's Socialist Economy (1979), went to a third
printing as of March 1981, with a total print size of
over 2 million copies. China's Socialist Economy has
been translated by the Foreign Languages Press in Beijing
into English, Japanese, and French. It is also being
translated into German in West Germany. His much earlier
work, the Socialist Transformation of the National
Economy in China, enjoyed similar international exposure
with its official English, Japanese, French, German, and
Spanish editions.

Since major state publishing companies in China are
presumably under the strict control of the Chinese
Communist Party, Xue's successful publishing records
would not have been possible without at least tacit official blessings. However, the course of Xue's career was
not always this smooth. When his views ran counter to
the official positions in the Cultural Revolution, he was
branded as a counter-revolutionary revisionist and
purged.[2]

III. SUMMARY OF CURRENT ECONOMIC PROBLEMS

A. Causes of current problems

According to Xue, the current economic problems in
China resulted from an uncritical imitation of the overly
centralized and excessively rigid economic management
system as practiced in the Soviet Union in the 1950s.
This system was characterized by excessive command
planning and overemphasis on capital formation.

To facilitate command planning in China, three stra-
tegies were adopted: (1) the economy was simplified to
reduce the number of economic linkages that need to be
considered, (2) power was centralized to ensure that economic policies were implemented without deviation, and
(3) feedbacks were suppressed by dissociating rewards and
punishments from performance to reduce the number of
adjustments that need to be made in the state plans.

To simplify the economy, the following measures were
adopted: First, ownership relations were advanced beyond
the development of productive forces. Many economic
activities were either eliminated because they could not
be easily collectivized or prematurely collectivized.
Those that were collectivized were prematurely forced
into bigger collective ownership or whole people
ownership.

Second, the number of circulation channels was
reduced. Trade in the rural areas was monopolized by
supply and marketing cooperatives. Trade in the urban

areas was monopolized by state commerce departments. Foreign trade was monopolized by the Ministry of Foreign Trade. And the plan allocation of producer goods was handled by a separate network under the direction of material resources departments.

To centralize control, the following measures were taken: First, plan targets set by the Central government were dictated to local authorities and enterprises regardless of their suitability.

Second, fiscal revenues were centralized. Most taxes, all profits, and most of the depreciation charges of state enterprises were delivered to the Central government.[3]

Third, fiscal expenditures were centralized. Most capital and current expenditures of local authorities, institutions, and state enterprises were financed by the Central government. All budgeted expenses had to be used as designated.

Fourth, state enterprises were put under the control of government organs which made all the important management decisions for them.

Fifth, labor and scarce consumer and producer goods were centrally allocated.

To suppress feedbacks, the following measures were adopted: First, prices were determined according to subjective wishes rather than supply and demand conditions.

Second, enterprise performance was evaluated not by profits or losses but by the fulfillment of gross output targets.

Third, funds for capital and current expenditures were allocated to state enterprises interest-free regardless of profits or losses.

Fourth, the urban labor force and scarce consumer and producer goods were allocated with little regard to needs, preferences, or skills.

Fifth, all state enterprises followed the same pay scales regardless of their fulfillment of the output targets and their contribution to the state.[4] All staff and workers in the same pay grades were treated equally regardless of the quantity and quality of their work. There were no demotions or firings for poor performance and no promotions for good performance.

B. Effects

Simplifications of the economy, centralization of control, and suppression of feedbacks led to many problems, the most serious of which were:

1. Proportional imbalances in the economy. There was imbalance between investment and consumption with too much emphasis on investment. There was imbalance between

agriculture, light industry, and heavy industry with too
much emphasis on heavy industry. And there were imbalances within each of these three sectors. Within
heavy industry, there was too much emphasis on iron and
steel and not enough on coal, electricity, transportation, lumber, and cement. Within light industry,
arbitrary plan prices led to overproduction of abundant
products and underproduction of scarce products. Within
agriculture, there was too much emphasis on food grain
and not enough on agricultural sideline products.

2. Imbalances in budget, credit, and supplies. The
above-mentioned proportional imbalances were further
aggravated by chronic budget deficits financed by credit
expansion. Normally, capital investments were provided
entirely in the form of state allocations, as was quota
circulating capital. Banks were mainly responsible for
the extension of loans to cover circulating capital
needed in the exchange of products. If the circulation
of commodities had been smoothly carried out, the
repayment of loans when the goods were sold should have
balanced the extension of new loans. But when the
controls on bank loans were lax, bank loans often became
a source of funds to finance budget revenues. This happened when bank loans were tied up in stockpiles of
goods. Thus, state revenues could be inflated when the
producers delivered the profits from the sale of these
products to the commerce and material resources departments but before the goods could be sold to users and
the loans repaid.[5] As these stockpiled goods were not
likely to be sold and used immediately because they were
either defective, products that did not meet user needs,
or hoarded by users due to chronic shortages, credit
imbalances led to imbalances in supplies. If these
inflated state revenues were used for capital investment,
the projects would be held up due to shortages of producer goods. If they were used for wages, there would be
a shortage of consumer goods.

3. Overproduction of abundant products and
underproduction of scarce products. Since production
units could not market their products independently,
there was no way for them to judge market demand. They
therefore tended to produce products that commanded high
profit and as much of these products as the purchasing
departments were prepared to purchase. But since plan
prices and tax rates did not in general reflect scarcity,
there was chronic overproduction of some goods and
underproduction of others.

4. Underproduction in increasing-cost industries
and overproduction in decreasing-cost industries. Since
plan prices were adjusted only infrequently, if at all,
the spread between plan prices and production costs for
increasing-cost industries (such as agriculture and

mining) was increasingly reduced or eliminated. On the other hand, this spread was increasingly expanded for decreasing-cost industries (such as manufacturing). As a result, there was little incentive to expand output in increasing-cost industries.

5. Waste of capital funds. Since all profits of state enterprises had to be delivered to higher authorities and all expenditures (except extra-quota circulating capital) were provided interest-free by the higher authorities regardless of enterprise performance, there was no incentive to earn extra profits or reduce expenditures. In particular, enterprises all wanted to have a larger share of the funds for capital projects regardless of their soundness. As a result, many projects had long gestation periods due to non-availability of continuing financial and material supports. Many of these that were completed were not cost effective because they were not compatible with existing technical or economic conditions.[6]

6. Economic management by administrative rather than economic considerations. Since all enterprises under the whole people ownership were directly under the control of state or local governments, enterprises were run to benefit the administrative units which the enterprises happened to belong to. If they were controlled by Central ministries, the economic linkages between enterprises under different ministries would be severed. If they were controlled by local governments, the economic linkages between enterprises under different regional governments would be severed. This, together with other reasons, resulted in excessive duplication of production facilities, departmentalism, irrational circulation patterns, pursuit of local or departmental self-sufficiency, and hoarding of scarce producer goods.

7. Poor product quality, wrong output mix, and high production costs. Preoccupation with the high-speed growth of gross output, inappropriate prices, and limited capacity of state plans to accommodate variety all contributed to low production efficiency.[7]

8. Waste of manpower. To simplify their jobs, labor departments often placed job seekers with little regard for their capabilities and the needs of the employers. As a result, state enterprises were saddled with labor they did not need but were powerless to fire. Government departments and public institutions were similarly overstaffed. The most serious misallocation related to scientific and technical personnel. Many of these were hoarded by scientific research institutes where they had little or nothing to do but were not free to go if they found suitable jobs elsewhere.[8]

9. Reduction of services and employment opportunities. The elimination of small service industries

(such as restaurants, laundries, repair shops, retail
shops, peddling, short-haul transportation, etc.) in
urban areas imposed inconveniences on people's livelihood
and reduced employment opportunities.
    10. Discouragement of diversity. Commune and bri-
gade enterprises and other extra-plan activities could
not flourish because of state monopoly in the allocation
of producer goods and in the marketing of products.
Those that managed to develop were soon stifled as they
were absorbed into the rigidly planned economy.

    C. Current reforms

    Since the pre-reform problems resulted from too much
command planning and overemphasis on capital formation,
the remedies adopted were mostly aimed at reducing the
scope of command planning and the level of capital formation. Some of these responses were still in an experimental stage limited to selected pilot projects.
    To reduce the scope of command planning, centralized
and exclusive control over income distribution and commodity circulation was relaxed. In the area of income
distribution, the following measures were tried:
    1. State enterprises were allowed to retain part of
their profits to be used on capital investment and
employee welfare. In exchange, enterprises had to be
responsible for their profits and losses. They also had
to pay interest for use of fixed and circulating capital.
    2. Local governments were allowed to share tax
revenues and enterprise profits with the Central government. With these decentralized funds, local governments
could make their expenditure decisions to better suit
local conditions. In exchange, local governments had to
balance their budgets without assistance from the Central
government.[9]
    In the area of commodity circulation, the following
steps were taken:
    1. Commerce departments no longer had to purchase
whatever was produced by enterprises. Instead, they
could selectively purchase according to supply and demand
conditions.
    2. Enterprises could market independently whatever
was not purchased by commerce departments.
    3. Order-placing conferences and trade fairs were
organized to facilitate circulation of producer goods.
    4. Negotiated prices, coordination prices, and
farmers' market prices were allowed to deviate from plan
prices.
    5. Farmers' markets were opened up to allow
peasants to sell their surplus agricultural and sideline
products to urban residents.

6. Communes and brigades were allowed to sell their surplus products directly to urban areas.

To reduce capital formation and improve people's livelihood, the following steps were taken:

1. Capital construction undertaken by the Central government was reduced.

2. Wages for staff and workers were increased.

3. Purchase prices for agricultural products were increased while selling prices were not increased. The excess of purchase prices over selling prices was subsidized by the Central government.

D. Problems encountered in current reforms

In a healthy economy, there must be a balance between macro-compatibility (proportional balance) and micro-flexibilty. Micro-flexibility requires prices to reflect scarcity and freedom of producers and consumers to make decisions. In the absence of proportional balance (macro-compatibility) between consumption and investment, between and within industries, scarcity-determined prices and freedom of choice create serious equity problems. This is the dilemma faced by China today. Macro-compatibility had to be restored before micro-flexibility could be pursued to any significant extent. But lack of micro-flexibility also contributed to lack of macro-compatibility in the first place. Current reforms attempted to gradually introduce micro-flexibility while macro-compatibility was restored. But the difficulty in maintaining a delicate balance between macro-compatibility and micro-flexibility, and between equity and efficiency, explains many of the problems encountered in current reforms.

Decentralization of power through reform in income distribution ran into the following problems:

1. Profit retention in state enterprises did not lead to financial accountability, because prices and tax rates were not adjusted. Prices that did not reflect scarcity and tax rates that did not offset differential rent meant that the financial status of enterprises did not reflect their performance. Inappropriate prices and tax rates also led to shortages of raw materials, fuels, and power, which made fulfillment of production targets impossible. Instead of changing prices, the profit retention ratio was set to vary inversely with existing profits to even out hardship and joy among enterprises. But this temporary measure made it more difficult to adjust prices later on.

2. Financial accountability of enterprises was also hampered by the lack of power to hire or fire personnel and the accumulated advantage of past uncompensated use

of fixed assets.   Enterprises with more investment and
better equipment naturally enjoyed a higher labor productivity with higher profit.   But compensated use of fixed
assets could not begin without a nationwide appraisal of
fixed assets of state enterprises in the first place.[10]
     3. Fiscal   independence   of   local   governments
destroyed both macro-compatibility and micro-flexibility
because the administrative structure was not separated
from the economic structure.   Specifically, it induced
(a) independent local capital investment which more than
offset the reduction of capital investment by the Central
government, (b) excessive local interference with
enterprise management in order to increase the profit
share going to local governments, and (c) local self-
sufficiency rather than development of comparative
advantage.
     Reform in commodity circulation ran into the
following difficulties:
     1. Exchanges conducted outside the state monopoly
commercial network threatened the stability of plan
prices by exposing the serious deviation of plan prices
from opportunity costs and diverted resources from their
planned allocations.
     2. Financial independence of local governments
abetted the development of self-sufficiency and departmentalism, and limited the scope of reform in commodity
circulation across administrative boundaries.
     Adjustments of economic levers ran into the
following difficulties:
     1. Selective upward adjustments of some plan prices
put pressure on other plan prices that had not been
adjusted.   As resources were diverted from the production
of products with unadjusted prices to the production of
products with adjusted prices, the incidence of scarcity
shifted.
     2. Raising the purchase prices without raising the
selling prices, as in the case of food grain, edible
oils, and cotton, succeeded in raising output and the
welfare of the producers without adversely affecting the
welfare of the users, but at the expense of budgetary
balance.   The excess of purchase prices over selling
prices also meant that prices for food grain sold to
urban residents were lower than those charged to the
rural producers.[11]
     3. Prices for many scarce producer goods, such as
coal and lumber, could not be raised because production
costs of users and costs of living would go up.
     4. Across-the-board distribution of wage increases,
bonuses, and promotions failed to create incentives for
higher labor productivity.   Instead, enterprises with a
large payroll and low labor productivity due to excess
labor benefited.   This problem could not be solved until

enterprises were given more power to determine personnel and wage matters.

Retrenchment in capital formation by Central government ran into the following difficulties:

1. In heavy industry where retrenchment was successful, unemployment was the result.

2. Investments in many capital projects were already committed and could not be terminated right away.

3. Retrenchment by Central government was partly offset by expansion at the local levels.

E. Successes in current reforms

Most of the successes were achieved in the area of commodity circulation. They were:

1. Selective purchase by commerce departments reduced inventory of unwanted products.

2. The reopening of farmers' markets stimulated the production of subsidiary foodstuffs and other sideline products.

3. Order-placing conferences and trade fairs for producer goods reduced hoarding of producer goods.

4. Independent marketing by enterprises permitted direct contact between producers and users.

5. Production according to sales replaced sales according to production.

6. Negotiated prices, coordination prices, and farmers' market prices revealed the extent plan prices deviated from market prices and should facilitate future adjustment of plan prices.

Retrenchment of capital formation by the Central government also produced benefits:

1. Surplus capacity in heavy industry encouraged the production of extra-plan products that were much needed but were ignored when capital formation was overextended.

2. Lower demand for machines and steel products permitted the redirection of attention from plan allocation to marketing.

F. Proposals for future reforms

Xue affirmed the directions of current reforms and wanted them to be extended beyond their experimental stage. However, he thought that redistribution of revenues between the Central government, local governments, and state enterprises without separating the economy from the government structure would not lead to greater economic efficiency. Unless the economy was managed by economic measures rather than administrative fiats, decentralization of financial power would simply create more freedom to suboptimize. While Xue still insisted that planning was necessary to realize the superiority of the socialist system, he thought that the planned targets must largely be realized through the market if inefficiency was to be avoided.

Thus, the roles played by government organs of economic administration would have to be changed. Specifically:

1. Government agencies should be disengaged from enterprises so that they only ensure adherence by enterprises to goals and policies for developing the national economy, and do not interfere with concrete economic activities for their departmental interests.

2. Command planning should be reduced as supply and demand conditions become more favorable.[12] But the state must still control the relation between investment and consumption to ensure proportional balance.

3. Where command planning is still needed, product variety, specifications, and colors should be determined by producers and buyers according to market requirements.[13]

4. Where supply and demand conditions permit, reference targets should be used and enterprises should be left alone to make concrete arrangements.[14]

5. Economic levers, such as prices, tax rates, and interest rates, rather than administrative fiats should be used to ensure fulfillment of reference targets.[15]

6. Price departments should not set concrete prices. Instead, they should only determine policies of price adjustment and supervise and guide prices.

7. Where concrete prices must still be set for scarce goods, standard prices should be sufficient. Detailed prices should be set by specialized companies.

8. Banks should be allowed to adjust interest rates and credit policy to direct enterprise development instead of being cashier agencies for the Ministry of Finance. They could also facilitate commodity circulation by reviving commercial credit arrangements.

If the market was to be used to improve allocative efficiency, any obstacles to market competition had to be removed or the wrong kind of market signals would be generated, leading to inefficient resource allocation. Specifically:

1. Monopoly in commodity circulation should be further reduced by allowing producers (state, collective, or individual) to market their surplus products directly to users across administrative boundaries. The scope of plan allocation of producer goods should be reduced. And commercial institutions such as warehousing, commercial agents, exchanges, and other commercial organizations should be revived.

2. Economic incentives should be related to performance. Poor performance should be punished and good performance should be rewarded.

3. Protective economic barriers between industries and regions should be broken down.

4. Prices and tax rates should be set to eliminate shortages and surpluses and to encourage the production of new and/or high-quality products.

The separation of the economy from the administrative structure and the fostering of market competition would make it possible and necessary to develop joint ventures and comparative advantage. Specifically:

1. Joint ventures could be developed between producers and processors of raw materials, between users and producers of finished producer goods, between small producers specializing in spare parts and accessories and large producers specializing in assembled finished goods, and between intermediate processors and final processors of manufactured goods.

2. These joint ventures could increase output by emphasizing comparative advantages, reduce duplication of production facilities, avoid unnecessary competition for raw materials, power, and market outlets, and prevent wholesale bankruptcy of many small independent producers.

3. These joint ventures could be organized by trans-provincial companies based in large urban centers through investment and technical assistance.

4. Regional comparative advantage in agricultural, livestock, forestry, and fishery products could also be developed by abandoning policies of local self-sufficiency, adjusting prices, and ensuring supply of consumer goods.

5. Joint ventures and regional comparative advantage would revive traditional economic centers serving more than one administrative region and further divorce the economy from the administrative structure.

The close relation between the economy and the administrative structure and the circumvention of market regulation in China were, according to the Marxist dogma, ultimately justified by the ownership system. If means of production were owned by the whole people, then they should be managed by the state as the representative of the whole people. And if means of production were owned by the collective, then they should be managed by the collective as representative of its members. The ownership system, instead of being justified by the development of productive forces, was treated as a desirable end in itself regardless of the level of productive forces. And the higher the degree of public ownership, the better it was. Therefore, any vestiges of private ownership became suitable targets for elimination. This obsession with the form rather than the substance of ownership therefore had to be changed if the economy was not to be strangled. Xue proposed the following remedies:

1. Collective ownership should be permitted within whole people ownership and individual ownership should be permitted within collective ownership.

2. Ownership should not dictate the mode of operation. For example, production team ownership in the rural areas should not preclude the assignment of production responsibility to the group, the household, or the individual wherever such arrangement could improve productivity.

3. Ownership should be determined by productive forces. For example, in the rural areas, although the production team was the basic unit of collective ownership, brigade ownership or even commune ownership might be appropriate where productive forces were sufficiently developed.

4. Production could be organized through supply and marketing networks rather than ownership reform, such as in agriculture.

5. Even in urban areas, there should be room for collective ownership, cooperative ownership, and individual ownership in the provision of consumer services.

IV. EVOLUTION OF XUE'S ECONOMIC VIEWS

Xue's critical views of China's economic management system as expressed in Current Economic Problems reflect both the climate of a more tolerant era and the maturing views of a seasoned observer of China's struggling socialist economy over its 30-year existence.

Before the Cultural Revolution, Xue was never sure whether the state and the market were competing or complementary forces in the regulation of economic activities. Consequently, he was not sure about the exact scopes of these two regulating forces. This lack of clarity apparently resulted from his confusion between the validity of the law of value (i.e., equilibrium prices should be set according to socially necessary labor) and the form in which the different functions of this law were performed under different social and historical conditions. The operation of the law of value through spontaneous market forces as in capitalist countries might have seemed to be unnecessarily wasteful and destructive to Xue. This aversion to spontaneous market forces might have inspired the desire to limit their scope. And limiting the scope of spontaneous market forces was somehow equated with limiting the scope of the law of value.

The following quotations from Xue's "Commodity Production and the Law of Value under the Socialist System" (Red Flag, No. 10, 1959) are typical examples of this confusion.

> Lightning in the sky occurs spontaneously, while electricity in an electric light is under the command of the people. But if you violate the natural law of electricity, even electricity under people's control can still electrocute people and burn up buildings against people's wishes. The law of value is much like it. . . .
>
> . . . .
>
> Of course, we do not favor overestimating the function of the law of value. . . .
>
> . . . .
>
> On this question about the function of the law of value, if the law of value is unlimitedly used to regulate production and sales in place of state planning, as modern revisionists suggest, this is obviously a mistake. . . .[16]

Again, in his "Some Comments on Commodity Production and the Law of Value" (Economic Research, No. 1, 1959), he said:

> With respect to the question of whether the law of value will still play an important role in the future, I think the role of the law of value will be more restricted than in the previous period. . . .[17]

In Current Economic Problems, Xue finally decided that the law of value should apply both to the state and to the market. The following quotation is typical of his current views:

> In the past, it was thought that regulation through the market cannot be used simultaneously with regulation through planning. This is wrong. Plan regulation and market regulation should be used together and plan regulation should be realized largely through market regulation. . . .[18]

Xue also thought that the scope of state actions should be limited to indicative planning and manipulating incentives, thus:

> When imbalance in the national economy is successfully redressed in the future and a balance between supply and demand is achieved, command targets can be reduced to a minimum. The state will provide reference targets and market information will be

provided by economic levers: price policy, tax
policy, and bank credit policy, etc. . . .[19]

V.   REVISIONISM OR REINTERPRETATION?

Although Xue's views were more comprehensive than
those of most participants in China's current debate on
economic reform, they were by no means more radical. In
fact, judging from published articles in specialized
journals and symposiums, the general thrust of Xue's
views was widely shared by people in the economic circle.
Either for practical or ideological reasons, Xue,
like other critics of pre-reform economic policies, took
care to point out that his critique did not imply a
rejection of the Marxist ideology. Instead, he argued
that Marx was misinterpreted when his works were used to
justify pre-reform policies, particularly with respect to
the issues of ownership and commodity exchange.
To Xue, Marx's vision of a public ownership over all
means of production after the proletariat seized power
from the capitalists presumed that the proletarian revolution would win victory first in the most developed
capitalist country.   Therefore, the past tendency to
transform individual ownership into small collective
ownership, small collective ownership into big collective
ownership, and big collective ownership into whole people
ownership regardless of the development of productive
forces in China was a mistake. It reversed the normal
development process by imposing a set of production relations on the economy before it had developed the
appropriate productive forces.
Marx also speculated that in a socialist society
commodity exchange and money would no longer be
necessary. In such a society, the whole economy would be
an inseparable single entity. Its component parts would
have no individual interests apart from their common
interests. To most Chinese economists, this used to mean
that since products in a socialist society were no longer
commodities, they need not be exchanged at equal values.
Instead they could be allocated to where the planners
thought desirable regardless of opportunity costs.
The general neglect of opportunity costs in the
pricing of resources in China reflected this mode of
thinking. And the system of unified revenues and unified
expenditures in state enterprises further encouraged
uncompensated transfer of resources from more efficient
to less efficient enterprises. In their heyday, rural
people's communes were permitted to transfer labor and
other resources from their subordinate production units
at will without proper compensation.

Now, Xue and others argued that because there were still two ownership systems over means of production, exchange of products within the collective sector and between the collective sector and the whole people sector was definitely commodity exchange. Even within the whole people sector, because of uneven development among state enterprises, individual enterprises still had their independent and separate interests apart from the common interests. Exchange of products between enterprises must therefore still be accounted for, much like commodity exchange. This was made particularly obvious when the need for expanded enterprise autonomy was officially affirmed. There was no way enterprises could reasonably be made responsible for their profits and losses unless all transactions, including exchange of products, were fully accounted for in terms of opportunity costs. And when products were exchanged at opportunity costs, they were nothing but commodities.[20]

To Xue, commodities, money, prices, and market regulation were simply means to develop large-scale social production. Like Marx, he thought these historical categories would disappear once large-scale social production was achieved at the higher level of communism, although the calculation of socially necessary labor time would still be necessary.[21]

VI.   SYSTEM FAILURE OR SYSTEM MISMANAGEMENT?

Is the failure of the Chinese economy a failure of system or a failure of management? This is an intriguing question. If it is a failure of management, then better management would solve the problem. But if it is a failure of system, then only a change of the system can solve the problem. Xue seemed to think that it was a failure of system but did not attempt to analyze it in any theoretical framework. An appropriate theoretical framework would be most useful here, as it would draw out the general implications of China's current economic problems. Such a framework has already been well developed. Specifically, it is the conceptual framework of a cybernetic system.[22]

An economic system, like other cybernetic systems, is essentially a goal-seeking system. The system is more or less efficient depending on how well the chosen goals are satisfied given the resources. To determine how well the system as a whole or its subsystems are attaining their goals, the system needs to have interconnecting feedback loops. Feedback loops are of two kinds, negative and positive. When deviations from a norm set in motion forces which counteract and ultimately eliminate the deviations, we have a negative feedback loop.

Negative feedbacks thus stabilize the system at some chosen levels.   On the other hand, when desired (undesired) behavior is rewarded (punished), and the reward (punishment) varies directly with the extent of the desired (undesired) behavior, we have a positive feedback loop.   Positive feedbacks thus ensure loop selection, maintenance, and system expansion.

If feedback loops are to operate properly, the "actors" in the loops must receive accurate information or they will be led into unproductive activities.   The unrestricted market is the classic method to organize feedback loops because it determines prices and is in turn affected by prices.   Prices are simply signals indicating scarcity, shortages, and surpluses.   When shortages occur, prices rise to induce higher output.   As output increases, prices fall.   In this adjustment process, both negative and positive feedbacks are involved. The tendency towards a market equilibrium is obviously an example of negative feedback.   Shortages and surpluses set in motion forces for their elimination.   But if higher output is rewarded with higher profit when shortages occur, and if lower output is rewarded with lower losses when surpluses occur, positive feedbacks are also at work.

When positive feedback loops are supplied with the wrong information, positive feedbacks become disruptive and system equilibrium can no longer be maintained.   For example, if higher output is rewarded with higher profit when surpluses occur or if lower output is rewarded with lower losses when shortages occur, shortages and surpluses will persist and intensify.

Through competition, the market also encourages excess creation.   Market selection among these alternatives ensures that the most system-compatible activities survive and are incorporated into the feedback system. System compatibility implies that each available niche in the economy is filled by the most efficient producer.   Therefore, any attempt to reduce competition may lead to unfilled niches and/or niches that are filled by less efficient producers.

The market is useful in loop selection, maintenance, and system expansion in a world of uncertainty.   It is a device for information search.   In a world of perfect foresight and knowledge, loops can be selected, maintained, and expanded with certainty.   The waste of resources connected with excess creation and selection through trial and error in the market would be unnecessary.

The problem with command central planning lies in the fact that an artificially determined system of feedback loops and feedback signals is imposed on the economy in a world with far less than perfect knowledge and

foresight. The irony is that command central planning is
seldom practised in a static economy where the chance of
its success is the highest.   In a static economy with a
constant flow of resources, all niches would be filled by
the most efficient producers through repeated trial and
error.   And with perfect knowledge, command planning
would be easy--but, by the same token, unnecessary.   On
the other hand, in an economy aspiring to growth, the
increasing flow of resources constantly creates new
niches to be filled.   Here, however, command planning is
least likely to be successful because of uncertainty.
And yet it is here that command central planning is most
frequently practised.[23]
     The purpose of central planning is, of course, to
artificially rearrange feedback loops so that they can
set the economy growing along a path of non-disruptive
positive feedback.   Indeed, all political revolutions
must ultimately be justified by the mandate to rearrange
disruptive feedback loops into non-disruptive feedback
loops.   That the market by itself cannot properly induce
all the necessary feedback loops for economic growth
whenever feedbacks are indirect and distant is well
known.   For example, where infrastructural investment
projects have long gestation periods with non-excludable
benefits, the market cannot in general be depended upon
to undertake them.   Nor can the market redistribute
wealth (in contrast to income) efficiently.   The problem
of central planning is not that the market is circum-
vented in those areas which central planning can in principle carry out more efficiently than the market, but
that central planning often goes beyond its areas of com-
petence and encroaches upon areas where the market is
more efficient in arranging feedback loops.
     However, no feedback system can ignore feedbacks
forever.   System-incompatible feedback loops sooner or
later will manifest their incompatibilities.   When these
are revealed and ignored, it is necessary to explain why
the system fails to take notice and take action to
correct them.   Thus, command central planning may have
been ineffective in selecting proper feedback loops
because of uncertainty and imperfect foresight.   But when
information is generated by feedbacks, why doesn't the
planning apparatus take advantage of it?
     Here, it is important to remember that command
central planning in China was carried out by a monolithic
bureaucracy.   What is more, this bureaucracy had direct
and indirect control over all means of production and all
spheres of economic activities.   Indeed, the economy was
part of this monolithic bureaucracy.   In terms of feedback system analysis, bureaucracies are non-adaptable
feedback loops.   They are usually created for some speci-
fic goals.   And to ensure the attainment of these goals,

strict budgetary and administrative procedures are insti-
tuted.   These institutional rigidities, while ensuring
accountability, also deprive bureaucracies of the flexibility in resource use that is needed to search for
better ways to achieve the specified goals or to redefine
their goals under changing conditions.   Typically, there
are no budgetary provisions for non-specific items.   And
savings obtained from one budget category due to efficiency are generally not transferable to another.[24]
    Since bureaucracies are pervasive in public and pri-
vate sectors of all economies whenever a certain scale of
operation is exceeded, they are not in themselves a
problem.   The problem is that whenever there is no market
test or competition in general to determine the efficiency of alternative bureaucratic structures, there is
no mechanism to force adjustment of existing ones or to
select more efficient alternatives.   It is this lack of
loop adjustment and selection mechanism that explains the
origin of departmentalism, the most serious of bureaucratic defects.   Thus, rearrangements of feedback loops
that can easily increase economic efficiency are usually
not carried out because departmental boundaries have to
be crossed.
    A monolithic bureaucracy that covers all spheres of
economic activities ensures that such a market test is
hard to come by.   At the policy-making level, such
responses are of course possible.   But in a single-party
system, if the party leaders decide to ignore the
unpleasant feedbacks for practical or ideological
reasons, there is often no institutionalized means for
their competitors to assume power in order to effect the
necessary changes.   And when such a change of power
finally occurs, the problem usually has deteriorated too
much to permit easy solutions.
    Xue's Current Economic Problems explains the struc-
ture of China's monolithic bureaucracy as it relates to
the economy and its inefficiencies, and suggests ways to
release the economy from the stranglehold of this
bureaucratic structure.   Xue's papers are as fascinating
as they are reassuring.   They describe views which,
though not always new, have never been told in such a
coherent manner or by a person of such high official
position.   And they confirm the worst of what many
thinking people have long suspected of the Chinese economy.   But Current Economic Problems perhaps assumes
greater significance as a case study of the general relationship between feedback systems and political/economic
structures, particularly with respect to the market and
the bureaucracy.

VII. SIGNIFICANCE

Current Economic Problems in China has successfully challenged the orthodox understanding of what a planned socialist economy should be doing. Western readers will be relieved to find that even "utopia" is not exempt from economic laws.

By exposing the shortcomings of China's planned socialist economy, Current Economic Problems will embarrass a lot of China experts who saw the pre-reform Chinese way of economic development as a model for other Third World countries to emulate and who uncritically accepted much of the now bankrupt official positions. Even if the present economic reforms are later reversed, the damage done to the myth of incomparable superiority of the orthodox socialist system can never be undone.

Since many of the policy proposals in Current Economic Problems have not been carried out, they provide a crystal ball to China's probable economic course if the present trend towards economic liberalization continues. The implications for scholarly research and business opportunities in China can hardly be exaggerated.

K. K. Fung

NOTES

1. Xue Muqiao, China's Socialist Economy (Beijing: Foreign Languages Press, 1981), p. 316.
2. Wolfgang Bartke, Who's Who in the People's Republic of China (Armonk, New York: M. E. Sharpe, Inc., 1981), p. 447.
3. Xue, China's Socialist Economy, p. 204.
4. Ibid., p. 87.
5. Ibid., p. 192.
6. Ibid., pp. 199-200.
7. Ibid., pp. 197-198.
8. Ibid., p. 201, pp. 215-217.
9. Ibid., p. 220.
10. Ibid., p. 231.
11. Ibid., pp. 148-149.
12. Xue Muqiao, "Plan Regulation and Market Regulation," in Current Economic Problems in China (Beijing: People's Publishing Company, 1980), p. 250. To avoid excessive duplication in content, this paper is not included in the present volume.
13. Ibid., p. 249.
14. Ibid., p. 250.
15. Ibid.

16. As quoted in Sun Yefang, "On Value," <u>Some Theoretical Issues in Socialist Economics,</u> ed. and trans. by K. K. Fung (Armonk, New York: M. E. Sharpe, Inc., 1982).

17. <u>Ibid</u>.

18. <u>Xue</u>, "Plan Regulation and Market Regulation," p. 250.

19. <u>Ibid</u>.

20. <u>Ibid</u>., p. 243.

21. <u>Xue, China's Socialist Economy</u>, p. 133.

22. Howard T. Odum, <u>Environment, Power, and Society</u> (New York: Wiley – Interscience, 1971); M. Maruyama, "The Second Cybernetics: Deviation-Amplifying Mutual Causal Processes," <u>American Scientist</u>, vol. 51 (1963), pp. 164–179.

23. K. K. Fung, "On Romantic Love – An Analysis of Open System Behavior," <u>Policy Sciences</u>, vol. 11, no. 2 (1979), pp. 179–186.

24. Robert K. Merton, "Bureaucratic Structure and Personality," in <u>Reader in Bureaucracy</u>, ed. by Robert K. Merton <u>et al</u>. (New York: The Free Press, 1952), pp. 361–371.

Editorial Notes

1. In the translated text, an asterisk before a number in superscript indicates an editor's note.

2. Where necessary, a term will be explained by a note at its first occurrence. This note will not be referred to by further notes at later appearances of the same term. Instead, it can be located through the index.

3. All names of persons and places are rendered in the official Chinese Pin-Yin system.

4. A table of contents of the Chinese edition is provided in Appendix A to indicate what has been included in or excluded from the English edition.

5. Dates of frequently mentioned events are listed in a separate table (Appendix B).

6. Chinese units of measurement are converted into American units in a conversion table (Appendix C).

Acknowledgments

1. Xue Muqiao for his permission to translate Current Economic Problems in China and for his approval of my selections for the English edition.

2. Leslie Burkett, of the Bureau of Business and Economic Research, Memphis State University, for her copyediting.

3. Lynn Haboush for typing the first draft and Janice Cook for preparing the final camera-ready copy on a word-processor.

K. K. Fung
Department of Economics
Memphis State University

Author's Preface

China's Socialist Economy,*1 which I wrote with the help of several comrades, has been published for one year. In this one year, many new developments have occurred in China's socialist economic construction, both in theory and in practice. This summer, the Ministry of Education convened a study conference on political theory. I originally intended to invite opinions about this book from participating teachers of political economy from various places so that necessary changes could be made. Later I discovered that many comrades could not get this book, so no discussion could be arranged. Also, I could not spare the time to revise it. So revision was postponed. At present, the People's Publishing Company is printing many more copies to enlarge distribution on the one hand. And it is also publishing a collection of my recent talks and papers to make up for the inadequacies in the earlier book.

In the past two years, I made more than ten reports on economic construction, especially on the system of economic management, and published some papers. In the editorial process, I found content repetition in some papers. I therefore got rid of several reports with excessive duplication and deleted parts of some papers. Even after this, there are still many repetitions. I must ask my readers for their indulgence. Also, the repeated contents were not all approached in the same way. My readers can decide on which are the better approaches. It should be pointed out that some views are still tentative even to myself. Also because of time limitation, I could not make changes with the full benefits of wide consultations. I hope my readers can treat them as "preliminary drafts."

Most problems touched upon in this book are still under study and discussion in the relevant departments. There will surely be new developments as time goes on. Since the Third Plenary Session of the Party's Eleventh Central Committee,*2 we have made rapid advances in our

1

economic theory and economic policies with our liberated minds. If a theorist wants to be ahead of his time in studying new conditions and solving new problems, he must not be afraid of making mistakes. He must be prepared to face the test of facts, constantly accept criticisms, and correct his mistakes. After reading these papers, my readers will easily find that there have been many developments and changes since the publication of my China's Socialist Economy a little more than a year ago. Even within this book, there are some changes from the beginning to the end. A person's thought should develop with time to avoid ossification. Of course, it cannot change with every direction of the wind. This is the principle that a scientist must hold on to. Some changes in this book resulted from my past mistakes, which hasty thinking made inevitable. I will be happy if only my basic direction is correct.

--Xue Muqiao
September 18, 1980

EDITOR'S NOTES

*1. Chinese edition was first published in December 1979 by the People's Publishing Company in Beijing. English edition was published in 1981 by the Foreign Languages Press in Beijing.
*2. The Third Plenary Session of the Chinese Communist Party's Eleventh Central Committee was held in December 1978.

1
Economic Work Must Be in Accordance with Laws of Economic Development

HIGH-SPEED AND PROPORTIONAL DEVELOPMENT OF THE SOCIALIST ECONOMY

The purpose of production in a socialist country is to satisfy the ever-increasing needs of the people. Since people's livelihood needs are constantly increasing, there is always the possible conflict of social production lagging behind social needs. Particularly with a country like ours which has a very low standard of living, this conflict is all the more noticeable. To resolve this conflict, we must develop production at high speed. Lenin thought that in order to expand reproduction on the basis of advanced technology, it was necessary to give priority to developing the production of producer goods. Therefore, Stalin placed special emphasis on the priority development of heavy industry in undertaking socialist economic construction. But if heavy industry develops too fast, it will inevitably hinder the development of agriculture and light industry because not only a lot of labor but also a lot of capital funds will be required to develop heavy industry. Overinvestment in heavy industry will inevitably squeeze agriculture and light industry. When agriculture and light industry are squeezed, they will develop too slowly. Not only will people's livelihood be threatened, but heavy industry will also be bogged down.

Thirty years' experience tells us that one important condition for high-speed development of the national economy is to properly handle the proportional relations among agriculture, light industry, and heavy industry. In 1956, comrade Mao Zedong in his "On the Ten Major

A Report to the Enterprise Management Study Group of the State Economic Commission, March 14, 1979.
This paper has three sections. Only the second section is translated here to avoid excessive duplication in content.--ed.

Relationships" already criticized Stalin's error of over-emphasizing heavy industry and neglecting agriculture and light industry.   Even after this criticism, we made an even greater mistake than the Soviet Union.   When the socialist transformation of the ownership of means of production was proceeding smoothly, we became over-confident and erroneously anticipated a historically unprecedented "Great Leap Forward."   The Program for Agricultural Development announced in 1955 originally allowed 12 years (1967) for its completion.   But many regions wanted to complete it in three to five years. Some unrealistic measures were suggested (such as making several million double-wheeled double-share plows). These were obviously unattainable at that time.   An editorial in the People's Daily warned people against day-dreaming and trying to do what was impossible.   The editorial received severe criticisms.   During the Spring Festival of 1958, emergency conferences were convened to criticize "anti-rashness."   It was decided that "anti-rashness" would no longer be allowed in the future.   This criticism against "anti-rashness" led to the big rash advance of 1958.

In our First Five-Year Plan period, the growth rates of industrial and agricultural output were all very fast. There was a steady increase year after year.   In these five years, industrial output grew by an annual average of 18%, of which heavy industry grew annually by 25.4%, and light industry grew annually by 12.9%.   Agricultural output grew by an average of 4.5%.   In general, heavy industry grew slightly too fast, and agriculture grew slightly too slowly.   But there was still no proportional imbalance.   In the first half of 1958, industrial and agricultural production was in excellent shape to start with.   The original plan for steel output was 6.2 million tons.   With extra efforts, 7 million tons could be produced.   But the Ministry of Metallurgy proposed to increase it to 8 million tons.   In the Beidaihe Conference[*1] of this year, some comrades proposed to double the steel output from the 5.35 million tons of 1957 to 10.7 million tons.   The plan to increase the output of food grain was even more strange.   An experimental plot of land in Xin Li Village in the suburbs of Tianjin promised to produce more than 100,000 jin of food grain per mu.[*2]   Other fields promised to produce 5,000 to 10,000 jin per mu.   Several thousands of people visited them daily.   Most people were skeptical, but they dared not speak up for fear of being accused of "anti-rashness." Other regions were not content to be laggards.   The expected output of food grain reported by the various provinces of the country exceeded 1,000 billion jin.   The Beidaihe Conference estimated the output of food grain in that year to be at least 700 billion jin.   The figures of

700 billion _jin_ of food grain and 10.7 million tons of steel were even announced in the newspapers.

In order to complete the task of producing 10.7 million tons of steel, several tens of thousands of small blast furnaces were built overnight in the provinces. Later, iron was reportedly being smelted in kilns made for bricks, tiles, and lime, and steel was reportedly being smelted with indigenous methods. It degenerated into an open orchestration of falsehoods. Every day, the newspapers came up with myths of new records and fanned up typhoons of tall stories and lies. In the fall of this year, a telephone conference was convened to urge the provinces to complete the task of 10.7 million tons of steel. At that time, some comrades complained over the telephone that the iron smelted in small and big furnaces started by the masses using indigenous methods was completely useless. It was a waste of raw materials and fuels. They suggested that the planned target be reduced, or they would have to resort to falsification. But at the conclusion of the conference, the 10.7 million tons of steel was to be completed as planned, since the whole world already knew about the target. No words on falsification were ever mentioned. In the beginning of 1959, it was announced that steel output in 1958 reached 11 million tons, surpassing the target. In fact, only 8 million tons were useful. Of these, 400,000 tons were not up to the originally specified quality requirements. The announced output of food grain was 700 billion _jin_. After verification in 1959, it was reduced to 500 billion _jin_. Another verification in 1961 further reduced it to 400 billion _jin_. Because of excessive in-kind tax, compulsory purchase and "free meals," there was a famine in the rural areas in 1959.

At the time, everybody was still under the spell of an "exaggeration fever." In the winter of 1958, the planned output of steel for 1959 as reported by the provinces was set at 30 million tons. The State Planning Commission reduced it to 20 million tons. Comrade Chen Yun was concerned about this target and personally attended a conference at the State Planning Commission. He was quite happy to settle for 16 million tons. But his moderation fell upon deaf ears. Finally, the decision was to have an externally announced figure of 18 million tons, and an internal reference figure of 20 million tons. After two to three months, it was realized that 18 million tons was impossible to achieve. At the Shanghai Conference at the end of March 1959, the figure was changed to 16.5 million tons. At that time, some comrades said that 16.5 million tons was still too ambitious. But it would be difficult politically to reduce the figure any further. Comrade Mao Zedong made such a criticism at the conference: "I doubt that you comrades

in economic work really know any economics." He urged
comrade Chen Yun to reconsider his position. Comrade
Chen Yun suggested a reduction to 13 million tons. In
August of this year, comrade Zhou Enlai in his report to
the Standing Committee of the National People's Congress
suggested a revision of plan and statistical figures.
Steel output in 1958 was changed to 8 million tons. The
planned figure of 1959 was changed to 12 million tons
(50% higher than the 1958 revised figure). Output of
food grain for 1958 was changed to 500 billion jin. The
planned figure for 1959 was changed to 550 billion jin.
In that year, output of steel barely exceeded 13 million
tons after much blind effort. Output of food grain was
340 billion jin, a reduction of 15% over 1958.

The substantial drop in food grain production in
the three years between 1959 and 1961 was attributed to
severe natural calamities at that time. It now appears
that the main reason was the "communist fever" mentioned
earlier. In addition, there was the "exaggeration fever"
which overestimated output substantially. Excessive tax
and purchase based on these inflated figures overtaxed
the agricultural sector and substantially reduced the
activism of the peasants. Agricultural production did
not recover until the "60 Articles"[*3] of the people's
communes were announced and the quotas of tax and
purchase reduced in 1962.

Starting in 1959, there was a drop in agricultural
output. Then a drop in light industrial output followed.
Output in heavy industry should have been reduced correspondingly. But at the Lushan Conference, "Right oppor-
tunism" was criticized. The tone of this criticism grew
more "Left" as the time went on. In 1960, a plan for 18
million tons of steel was again formulated, an increase
of 5 million tons over 1959, and 10 million tons over
1958. Comrade Chen Yun was concurrently director of the
State Construction Commission. He already favored a
reduction in output targets and retrenchment in capital
construction in 1959. But people were not receptive. It
seemed that their feverish heads just would not cool down
before some hardships were encountered. At that time,
under the threat of "anti-Right deviation," the State
Economic Commission continued to put forth highly
spirited slogans and encourage completion of planned
targets. At the end, steel output exceeded 18 million
tons, and coal output exceeded 390 million tons. But
these were battles of attrition won at the expense of
regular maintenance of machines and equipment and tunneling in the coal mines. The process of capital deple-
tion led to the collapse in 1961. In the summer of 1960,
comrade Li Fuchun saw that such a proportional imbalance
among agriculture, light industry, and heavy industry
could not be allowed to persist. He ordered us to draft

a proposal to adjust the proportional relations of the national economy. Comrade Zhou Enlai highly valued the proposals made by comrade Fuchun, and expanded "adjustment" to the policy of "adjustment, consolidation, enrichment, improvement." After Chairman Mao's approval in the winter of that year, it was issued as a Central document. But it was already too late. History had meted out merciless punishments on us.

Output in heavy industry dropped substantially in 1961 and 1962. Steel output in 1961 was more than 50% lower than the previous year. There was another 27% drop in 1962. Coal output in 1961 dropped by 30% over the previous year. There was a drop of more than 20% in 1962. Investment in capital construction represented 28% and 32% of the national income in 1959 and 1960, respectively. It represented only 12.3% and 7.4% of the national income in 1961 and 1962, respectively. Such big fluctuations in output and capital investment indicated that our national plans violated objective economic laws and were seriously flawed.

The Second Five-Year Plan was formulated under the guidance of comrades Zhou Enlai and Chen Yun as early as the summer of 1956. Premier Zhou wanted us to estimate the growth rate of output and the gross national income in the second five years, take care of the proportion between accumulation and consumption, calculate the total amount of investment in the five years, and take care of the proportional relations among agriculture, light industry, and heavy industry. After repeated discussion, the accumulation rate was set at 25%. Steel output was to be increased to 12 million tons, and output of food grain was to be increased to 500 billion jin by 1962. This plan was deliberated on and approved by the First Session of the Eighth National Party Congress. It now appears that this plan was correct. If it was so implemented, development of the national economy in the Second Five-Year Plan period would have been even better than in the First Five-Year Plan period. Regrettably, this "proposed Second Five-Year Plan" was cast aside when fever went to people's heads in 1958. Three years' "Great Leap Forward" was followed by two years' big retreat in heavy industrial output. Agricultural output started to decline from 1959. In 1960, the proportional relations among agriculture, light industry, and heavy industry were seriously out of balance. People's living standard suffered severe setbacks for three years. These mistakes would never have been made if the "proposed Second Five-Year Plan" was seriously implemented.

Adjustment work on the national economy was started in 1961 under the leadership of Premier Zhou and comrade Chen Yun. Several important measures were adopted to address the then existing conditions.

First, the number of staff and workers was reduced. Twenty million staff and workers newly recruited from the rural areas were sent back to the rural areas. They were transformed from laborers consuming commodity food grain to laborers producing food grain. From 1958 to 1960, because industrial production had developed too fast and capital construction was overextended, 25.5 million staff and workers had been newly added. At the same time, agricultural labor had been reduced by 23 million people. On top of this, construction on irrigation and water conservancy was too ambitious. As a result, there was an acute shortage of labor participating in current production. In the fall of 1958, a lot of food grain and cotton were left unharvested due to labor shortage. Bumper crops did not lead to bumper harvests. The return of 20 million laborers to the first line of agricultural production was effected without any incidents. It was a brilliant move.

Second, capital construction was retrenched. Work on up to 10,000 construction projects was stopped. Investment in capital construction in 1962 was 80% less than 1960. Up to 10,000 half-finished projects were stopped or scrapped. Losses were substantial. But there was no other way out. First, the Ministry of Finance ran out of money. Second, even if money were available, there were no machines, equipment, and construction materials. Furthermore, many projects were not scientifically designed. Even though the lesson from this bitter experience was purchased at tens of billions of yuan, our reluctance to criticize the "Great Leap Forward" and our short memory doomed us to a repetition of the "anti-Right deviation" as soon as the economy recovered. Every year we said we were going to retrench capital construction, but we kept extending our commitment to it. This bias still resists correction up to now.

Third, heavy industrial production was curtailed. At that time, heavy industrial production could not grow anyway, even if we wanted it to. After several years of blind effort to increase output, machines and equipment were in a state of disrepair. Also, there was no coking coal to smelt steel. Half of the big blast furnaces of Anshan Steel were laying idle. Recovery in the coal mines was even slower than the steel industry. Not only were machines and equipment in a state of disrepair, but also tunneling was behind for one to two years. Could this reduction be lessened? Yes. The way to do it was to stop operation of the tens of thousands of small blast furnaces and use the coal thus saved to keep the big blast furnaces at Anshan Steel going. But many comrades objected to this because they thought it was a mistake of line to stop the operation of small blast furnaces. They must be protected at all cost. Under the leadership of

Premier Zhou, we drafted a document for the Central Finance and Economics Group. It proposed a method of "selective preservation and suspension." All plants producing low-quality products with high consumption of raw materials and fuels were to be "closed, suspended, merged or re-directed." Later in the "Cultural Revolution," this "abandonment fever" was severely criticized. This criticism was ostensibly directed at Liu Shaoqi, but was really intended for Premier Zhou, for they also knew this document was drafted under the leadership of Premier Zhou.

After major adjustments, industrial and agricultural output started to bounce back in 1963. In formulating the 1964 plan, there were two different views in the State Planning Commission. One claimed that adjustment had been completed. The other claimed that it had not, and must be continued. When a report was sent to Premier Zhou, he not only affirmed the latter view but also said that adjustment had to be made for three more years until it could be completed in 1965. It now appears that Premier Zhou's view was entirely correct. Output of steel and coal returned to normalcy in 1965 and 1966. Now comrades in economic work all say that work in 1965 and 1966 was very smooth-going, because the proportional relations were returned to balance after several years of major adjustment.

The reason why I have spent so much time on the three-year "Great Leap Forward" and the five-year "major adjustment" is to illustrate one point. Namely, socialist economic construction must follow objective laws of economic development. Otherwise, it will be punished by history. High speed must be governed by proper proportions. And proper proportions are conditioned upon a correct state plan that follows objective laws of economic development. Not only must a plan be complete, it must also have built-in slacks to accommodate unexpected extra-plan needs. The First Five-Year Plan and the proposed Second Five-Year Plan basically followed objective economic laws. When fever went to people's heads in 1958, all these were cast aside and criticized as "passive balancing." The newly invented "active balancing" treated "steel as the key link." Unrealistically high targets of 10.7 million and 18 million tons of steel were set for other sectors to emulate. Everybody was thus forced to raise their targets. To ensure the fulfillment of these targets, the proportional relations in the national economy were destroyed by overextending capital construction. History has long ago passed its judgment on the economic work in this period. But in the "Cultural Revolution," Lin Biao and the "Gang of Four" reversed right and wrong. What was wrong was said to be right. And the correct line was

said to be the wrong line. Even after the "Gang of Four"
was smashed, the history of these several years was still
treated as a "forbidden zone" by everybody. As a result,
many mistakes were still left uncorrected in the past two
years. It seems that it is extremely necessary to sum up
the experience and lessons of these eight years. At
present, the national economy is still out of balance.
We are still overextended in capital construction and
heavy industry and overindebted to people's livelihood.
But many comrades are thinking only of leaping forward
and nothing about adjusting. Practice has shown that if
the proportional relations are not properly adjusted, and
if comprehensive balance is not properly taken care of,
there is no way for us to leap forward. We will fall
down as soon as we start leaping foward.
    Here, it is necessary to talk about an old problem.
Namely, the tendency to advocate "active balancing" and
criticize "passive balancing"; the tendency to advocate
"strong link balancing" and criticize "weak link balancing." Planning must, of course, be concerned with
tapping potentials and strengthening weak links so that
balance can be achieved at a higher level. But, if we
pay attention to only the strong links and neglect the
weak links, balance will surely be destroyed in our
attempt to force the weak links to emulate the strong
links, regardless of objective feasibility. At present,
our weak link in industrial production is electricity
(there are, of course, other areas). If we adopt strong
link balancing, many plants will not be supplied with
electricity for more than 100 days a year. Therefore,
the decisive factor is still the weak link, and not the
strong link. This is an objective law that cannot be
changed at will. No amount of criticism can demolish it.
You can criticize to death those who support actions
according to objective laws, but you cannot make these
laws disappear. On the contrary, you will be punished
by objective laws.
    Since our memories about the fluctuating and
stagnating production brought about by the sabotage of
Lin Biao and the "Gang of Four" in the "Cultural Revolution" are still fresh, I need not spend time talking
about it. What must be stressed, however, is the
seriousness of the proportional imbalance in the
national economy brought about by the sabotage of the
"Gang of Four." The adjustment in the past two years has
made substantial headway. But a determined effort to
adjust the proportional relations and take care of
comprehensive balance has not been made. As a result,
there is still a sizable gap in this year's plan that
needs to be adjusted. At present, the domestic and
international situations are excellent. We do have the
conditions to make our economy grow faster. But if our

feet are not on solid ground, we will fall down as soon as we go up. I think when the situation is excellent, a little more slacks can be built into the plan. Last year the planned steel output was 28 million tons. But the actual steel output exceeded it. There is nothing wrong with that. What we are afraid of are exaggerations, lies, actions that violate objective economic laws, and short memories about the experience and lessons from the three-year "Great Leap Forward" and five-year "major adjustment." I might have been too harsh in all these. And I welcome your criticisms.

EDITOR'S NOTES

*1. Beidaihe is the location of a number of historic meetings. It is situated in Hebei province. This Beidaihe Conference refers to the enlarged meeting of the Political Bureau of the Chinese Communist Party Central Committee held from August 17 to 30, 1958.

*2. The national average yield per mu of paddy rice (a staple food grain with the highest per unit area yield) was 356 jin in 1955 and 436 jin in 1974. See Kieran Broadbent, A Chinese/English Dictionary of China's Rural Economy (Farnham Royal, England: Commonwealth Agricultural Bureau, 1978), p. 249.

*3. The "60 Articles" established a three-level ownership with the production team as the basic unit of ownership, production and distribution.

2
Comprehensive Balance
in the National Economy

Socialist countries adopt planned management of their national economies. The primary tasks of planned management are to achieve comprehensive balance among various sectors of the national economy; make overall plans and take both national construction and people's livelihood needs into consideration, so that there is a relative balance between social production and social needs; and guarantee a high-speed and proportional development of the national economy.

When New China was just established, there still existed in China three basic economic elements. Namely, the socialist state economy, the private capitalist economy, and the individual economy. Under the then existing conditions, we still could not adopt planned management for the whole national economy. But it was all the same necessary to maintain a rough balance between supply of and demand for various important products. What methods did we use? We relied primarily on the law of value and the law of surplus value. We placed orders with private industries to make them produce according to national needs. The bourgeoisie wanted to make profit. Our orders guaranteed the capitalist 10% to 30% profit (including income tax, public accumulation fund, and welfare fund) on their capital. Profit was higher for scarce products which the nation needed or for which production lagged behind needs, and lower otherwise. Once the capitalists accepted the orders, they had to produce according to state requirements. With respect to the small peasant economy, we used the law of value. In other words, we used a price policy. We raised prices for products whose production we wanted to encourage and lowered prices otherwise. We were very good at using economic means. Output increased very fast at that time. Supply and demand were well matched. Supply of various

---

A Report to the Central Party School, July 11, 1979.

commodities (including food grain and cotton fabrics) was
freely available.   There were no queues or panic buying.
Why was balance between supply and demand achievable in
the economic recovery period when three types of economy
co-existed and not achievable when the three great
transformations*1 were basically completed and after
large-scale economic construction was started?   One of
the important reasons was that we had established a
planned management system and had not achieved comprehensive balance.

We started with the First Five-Year Plan in 1953.
Then we were faced with the first strategic choice.
Namely, should we first take care of national construction, particularly heavy industry construction, or should
we first take care of people's livelihood, particularly
peasants' livelihood?   The strategy in our Revolutionary
War was rural areas first and urban areas second.   Could
the strategy of our economic construction be agriculture
first, industry (heavy industry) second? We could reduce
peasants' tax burdens, let them recover and have a
decent life for a period of time, and then pursue heavy
industry on that basis.   But we were learning from the
Soviet Union then.   Under the guidance of experts from
the Soviet Union, we formulated a five-year plan.   We
followed the road taken by the Soviet Union.   That is, we
gave priority to the development of heavy industry.
Where did the capital funds for heavy industry come from?
We had to rely mainly on the peasants at that time,
because output from heavy industry represented only 8% of
the gross industrial and agricultural output.   Output
from light industry represented some 22%.   On the surface, it seemed that it could provide a sizable portion
of accumulation.   In fact, most of its raw materials came
from agriculture.   And most of its accumulation was
derived indirectly from the peasants through exchange of
unequal values.   Agricultural products were purchased at
low prices and industrial products were sold at high
prices. Agricultural output represented 70% of the gross
output.   In addition to accumulation indirectly obtained
from the peasants through exchange of unequal values, the
state also directly taxed and purchased a large amount
of food grain from the peasants to meet the needs of an
ever-expanding urban population in connection with the
fast industrial development.   Even then, the proportions
among agriculture, light industry, and heavy industry
were actually out of balance.   The remedy was to adopt
in-kind tax, unified purchase, and quota purchase with
respect to the peasants, and adopt quantitive rationing
for food grain, cotton fabrics, etc. with respect to
staff and workers.   Although these administrative
measures were necessary and produced positive effects at
that time, tax and purchase were excesive in two years,

thus adversely affecting the production activism of the peasants and reducing the growth rate of agricultural output. This policy was consistently followed after this, leading to a further deterioration of this balance year after year. At present, more than one-fourth of the urban need for food grain has to be imported. Even cotton, edible oil, and sugar have to be imported.

If we change our strategic policy, and first take care of agricultural production and peasants' livelihood, we can give a decent life to the peasants in three to five years with the spirit of the great Yenan production campaign. Marked development in agriculture can lead to marked development in light industry. With fiscal revenues greatly increased, not only can capital construction be increased, people's livelihood can also be improved. Then we do not have to run such a tight budget every year. Of course, we did achieve a great deal with the 156 items of capital construction in the First Five-Year Plan. We built the initial foundation for national industrialization. And all this is very important. Old China did not have much heavy industry. It was imperative that we undertook those capital construction projects. Therefore, it was correct that we did what we did in the First Five-Year Plan. The only problem was too much emphasis. In 1956, comrade Mao Zedong summed up the experience in his report "On the Ten Major Relationships." He criticized the Soviet Union for its one-sided emphasis on heavy industry to the neglect of agriculture. The problem was thus exposed. That year, the First Session of the Eighth National Party Congress approved the proposals for the Second Five-Year Plan. The accumulation rate was limited to 25%. (It was 24% in the First Five-Year Plan.) The growth rate of heavy industry was reduced appropriately, and the growth rate of agriculture was raised. From our present perspective, these adjustments were very appropriate. Regrettably, as soon as the Second Five-Year Plan was started (1958), there came a "Great Leap Forward." The 1958 annual steel output was to be doubled, at 10.7 million tons. The 1959 annual output was to be even higher, at 18 million tons. As a result, the balance among agriculture, light industry, and heavy industry was seriously disrupted. In three years, output from heavy industry was increased by more than two times. The accumulation rate reached about 40%. Agricultural output decreased by 25%. People's living standards deteriorated markedly. This crisis was only overcome after five years of adjustments.

When we say that the balance among agriculture, light industry, and heavy industry was restored in 1965 and 1966, we are talking in relation to the serious imbalance existing in the three-year "Great Leap Foward" period.

In fact, output from agriculture and light industry was still not high enough to meet the livelihood needs of the people. From 1956 to 1966, the average food consumption per capita of urban and rural residents was reduced from 409 jin to 381 jin--of which rural consumption was reduced from 410 jin to 373 jin. The average consumption of cotton fabrics per capita of urban and rural residents was reduced from 24.8 chi to 17.9 chi--of which rural consumption was reduced from 22.3 chi to 14.9 chi. At the same time, the share of accumulation in the national income exceeded 27% in 1965, and exceeded 30% in 1966. Thus, a new great leap forward was already emerging. Because we were afraid to tarnish the "three red banners,"*2 we did not seriously sum up the experience and lessons from the three-year "Great Leap Forward." Many problems were still tabooed. As a result, the imbalance among agriculture, light industry, and heavy industry could not be thoroughly corrected.

When the Third Five-Year Plan (1965-1970) was being formulated, two proposals were originally made. One was to peg the accumulation rate at about 25%. And steel output in 1970 was to be 18 million tons. The other was to peg the accumulation rate at about 30%, with steel output in 1970 at 20 million tons. After discussion, the second proposal was basically adopted. But the steel output was lowered to 16 million tons. From our present perspective, it would have been feasible to reach the steel output of 20 million tons (1966's output was already 15 million tons) if there had not been inter-ference from the "Cultural Revolution." Because of interference from the "Cultural Revolution" during the implementation of this plan, neither the plan for industrial production nor the plan for capital construc-tion was fulfilled. The actual accumulation rate in these five years was 26.3%. Because of substantial set-backs in 1967 and 1968, steel output did not even reach 18 million tons in 1970. In these years, the growth rate of agricultural output was not high either. Food con-sumption for urban and rural residents in 1970 was slightly higher than that of 1965 but slightly lower than that of 1966. Consumption of cotton fabrics was slightly increased. The Fourth Five-Year Plan (1971-1975) con-tinued the existing policy. The accumulation rate was increased to 33%. It was raised again to 36.5% in 1978, leading to further imbalance in the national economy. Imbalance in the national economy this time was, of course, to a large extent caused by the interference from Lin Biao and the "Gang of Four." But the emphasis on "steel as the key link" and the neglect of comprehensive balance by the planning agencies was also an important reason.

During the First Five-Year Plan period and when the Second Five-Year Plan was being formulated, the planning agencies paid frequent attention to comprehensive balance. From 1958 on, they no longer paid much attention to comprehensive balance. They criticized comprehensive balance as being "overcautious" and unnecesarily restrictive of the high-speed development of production. The new method of formulating plans was to highlight steel and to use steel to lead the other sectors. That is to say, a high output target was set for steel in order to force coal, electricity, transportation, etc. to catch up. This was thought to be a good method to develop the national economy at a high speed. But in order to raise the growth rates of these other sectors, it was necessary to expand the size of their capital construction. Consequently, the proportional relations between accumulation and consumption and the objective laws of economic development could no longer be of concern. It was thus all but inevitable that proportional imbalance in the national economy resulted. During the five-year adjustment period, this error was temporarily corrected. But the method of taking "steel as the key link" in formulating plans was left unchanged. Up to last year, the target of 60 million tons of steel in 1985 was still used as a benchmark in formulating the outline of the Ten-Year Plan. In order to achieve the target of 60 million tons of steel in 1985, it would be necessary to complete two to three Baoshan-sized steel plants in five to six years' time. In addition, output of coal, electricity, and transportation would also have to match this growth rate. Agriculture and light industry are therefore relegated to a residual status. Two years ago, it was already discovered that we had overextended ourselves in capital construction. Shortage of material resources was acute. But in order to ensure the fulfillment of 60 million tons of steel output, investment was increased several times. In 1978, appropriations for capital investment that were included in the state plan increased by 50% compared with the previous year. The actual realized capital investment reached 48 billion yuan (of which 40 billion were state investment), a 32% increase compared with the previous year. It was twice as fast as the growth rate of heavy industry (15.6%), and three and one-half times as fast as the growth rate of national income (12%). As a result, proportional imbalance in the national economy was further exposed.

In his report to the Second Session of the Fifth National People's Congress, comrade Hua Guofeng announced that we should use three years' time to adjust, reform, reorganize, and improve the national economy, and adjustment was to be the key to the overall situation of the national economy at the present time. To make

adjustment, we must first correctly handle the relations
between national construction and people's livelihood,
reduce our commitment to capital construction, and use
more funds to improve people's living standard so that
the peasants of the whole country can have a decent life.
That is to say, we have to adjust the proportional relations between accumulation and consumption, trying hard
to gradually reduce the accumulation rate from last
year's 36% to below 30%. This adjustment will also be
manifested as an adjustment of the proportional relations
among agriculture, light industry, and heavy industry.
We must accelerate in a big way agricultural development.
At the same time, we must accelerate the development of
light industry and meet the livelihood needs of the urban
and rural residents. In addition, we must adjust the
internal proportional relations within heavy industry,
develop fuels, electricity, and transportation, reduce
the growth rate of steel and machine-building industries,
and reduce the size of their capital construction. To do
a good job in comprehensive balance, the first thing to
do at present is to reduce the 60 million ton target of
steel output to 50 million tons or even 45 million tons.
In the past, we were suspended in mid-air by this 60
million ton output target. We were thus unable to pursue
comprehensive balance with our two feet on the ground.
If it is reduced to 45 million tons, then targets for
coal, electricity, and transportation can also be reduced. The tense situation existing in the national
economy may enjoy some relief as a result. After more
than 20 years of experience, if there is still no unified
understanding in the Party on this problem, and if we
still insist on maintaining the 60 million ton target of
steel output, then it will not be possible to pursue
comprehensive balance. And adjusting the proportional
relations becomes empty talk.

Six months have passed since the Center announced
the policy of adjusting the proportional relations of the
national economy. The State Planning Commission has done
a lot of work in relation to it. But judging from our
present conditions, adjustment has not produced significant results. Capital investment has only been temporarily braked. State appropriations for capital construction
have been reduced from 45 billion yuan to 36 billion
yuan. But up to now, most of these reductions are still
under negotiation. The number of items to be actually
retrenched is still very small. After retrenchment is
decided on, machines and equipment are still being built,
and staff and workers still receive wages. To avoid
conflicts, some provinces have reduced their investment
by the same proportion across the board. Overextended
items have not been retrenched and undercommitted items
have not been expanded. Most of the retrenchments are

merely postponements waiting to be revived at the first available opportunity. There are very few outright cancellations. In short, there has been strong resistance towards retrenchment in capital construction. This year, because of strong enforcement of existing policies and higher prices, agricultural output may increase at a high rate. In the first half of the year, light industry output fell short of the planned target (in the second half, it is rapidly growing). There has not been marked improvement in the proportional relations within heavy industry either. Therefore, we can only say that the three-year adjustment has just begun. In the next two years, a great deal of additional effort must still be made to complete this task.

The conditions for adjusting the national economy this time can be said to be much better than those existing in the 60's. During the last adjustment, output from industry and agriculture declined substantially. Output of food grain declined by 25%, output of coal declined by more than 40%, output of steel declined by more than 60%, and investment for capital construction declined by more than 80%. This time, agricultural output is increasing markedly. Industrial output is suffering a slight setback in its growth rate. Capital construction plus extra-plan investment are basically being maintained at last year's level. All this seems to be beyond dispute. But the reality is quite different. Last time, people were starving and realized that there was no other choice but to adjust. This time, living standards of urban and rural residents have not declined. This year, there may even be a slight improvement. Everybody says the situation is excellent. If the situation is so good, why are we still saying that there is proportional imbalance and that adjustment is necessary? Therefore, many comrades are still at a loss with respect to adjustment. Proportional imbalance in our national economy goes back a long time. People have long grown used to it. With 800 million peasants (of which 300 million are labor force), we still cannot solve the food problem. Supply of food grain and subsidiary foodstuffs is very short. Many peasants go hungry. Many comrades have long grown used to these conditions. They do not think that they are causes for alarm. If we are satisfied with our present conditions and pay attention only to our achievement to the neglect of inadequacies, we may be able to lead an uneventful life. But if we want to modernize in a down-to-earth manner, we must rack our brains and adjust the proportional relations with determination. To help our understanding, the following points must be clarified.

The first relates to how we should evaluate our present excellent conditions. In these two years, not only is our political situation excellent, our economic situation is also excellent. Agricultural output dropped in 1977. The reason was that most regions had not corrected the extreme Left line of the "Gang of Four" and policies had not been enforced. Industrial output grew at a high speed of 14.3%. In 1978, agricultural output increased at a high speed of 9%. Industrial output also grew at a high speed of 13.5%. These are indeed excellent situations which do not come by luck. But we should appreciate that these excellent situations are relative to the period during which the "Gang of Four" ran rampant. We saved the national economy from the brink of collapse and put it on the path towards the four modernizations.[*3]   Our achievements are indeed remarkable. But from the perspective of the past 30 years since the founding of the republic, particularly the past 20 years or so, we not only do not have anything to be proud of, we should instead feel ashamed of ourselves. We have not come up to the expectation of the workers and peasants of the whole country.

We still remember that during the three-year recovery, industrial and agricultural output both grew at a high rate. Industrial output grew at an average annual rate of 34.8%. And agricultural output grew an average annual rate of 14.1%. These were both high speeds. People's living standards improved markedly. People of the whole country were very happy. This was, of course, the high speed characteristic of recovery. In the First Five-Year Plan period, industrial output grew by an average annnual rate of 18%. Agricultural output grew by 4.5%. These high growth rates fully indicated the superiority of the socialist system. But in the last few years, cooperativization was proceeding a little too fast. The growth rate of agricultural output began to decline (7.6% in 1955; 5% in 1956, 3.6% in 1957, and 2.4% in 1958). In these five years, people's living standards continued to improve. The best year was 1956. Average per capita food grain consumption was 409 jin. This was reduced to 406 jin in 1957. The "Great Leap Forward" in the following three years brought about serious reduction in agricultural output and serious hardship to people's livelihood. Conditions started to regain normalcy only after five years of adjustment. Today, people miss the excellent conditions in 1965 and 1966. But they were excellent only relative to the preceding three years of hardship. In fact, the average per capita consumption of food grain was 368 jin in 1965 and 381 jin in 1966, much lower than the 409 jin of 1956 and 406 jin of 1957.

There were several ups and downs in agricultural production during the "Cultural Revolution." Newspapers claimed that agricultural output grew every year for more than ten years. These were lies. Food grain output

increased from 400 billion jin in 1958 to 570 billion jin
in 1976. Because of population increase, the average per
capita food grain consumption was only 383 jin, still
lower than 1956. The per capita food grain consumption
of peasants was reduced even more, from 410 jin to 372
jin. In 1978, output of food grain exceeded 600 billion
jin. The average per capita food grain consumption was
increased to 393 jin (385 jin for peasants), still lower
than 1956. Moreover, a lot of food grain was imported.
The average wages for staff and workers were 637 yuan in
1957, and 616 yuan in 1976 and 1977. They were increased
to 644 yuan in 1978, slightly higher than 1957. If the
increase in general price level is considered, it is difficult to say whether real wages had increased or
decreased. Isn't socialism supposed to be superior to
capitalism? If the living standard of workers and
peasants is not increased for a long time, people may
begin to wonder. We must strengthen ideological education to some youths who doubt the superiority of the
socialist system. But at the same time, we must do a
good job in building up our economy soon. Otherwise,
education alone is not convincing. Now many newspapers
frequently claim that the labor productivity, material
consumption, and profit of certain plants have equaled
the highest records in history. These so-called highest
records in history are mostly those existing before the
three-year "Great Leap Forward." In 20 years, other
people have advanced by big strides. But we have stopped
for 20 years. We should never be satisfied with these
conditions. And we have nothing to boast of.
     The second point relates to whether there is a pro-
portional imbalance and whether adjustment is necessary.
Many comrades think that we are short of everything now.
Since everything is short, it is not a matter of proportional imbalance. What we need is to go ahead at full
speed in all directions, and not adjustment. Of course,
we are behind in everything. And we must gather speed.
The question is whether we can catch up this way. We are
no longer youths. We have 30 years of experience behind
us. Wasn't the three-year "Great Leap Forward" a case of
full speed in all directions? Did we succeed in catching
up? We had to stop as soon as we started. Should we try
another of this "great leap forward"? We can't do it
anymore. If we try it once more, we will be behind
another 10 to 20 years. The people will not put up with
it. Shortages and surpluses are relative. Subjectively,
everything is short. Objectively, there can be shortages
and surpluses. For many years, under the influence of
the extreme Left line, we preferred to be "Left" rather
than "Right." The tendency was to identify the down-to-
earth attitude of doing things according to objective

laws as conservative thought, and to criticize it as such is too ingrained to be changed in a short time.

Recently, various departments have been discussing retrenchment of capital construction. They all claim that their departments are underfunded and need more funds. None of them claim that their departments are overfunded and need less funds. Take steel and machines as an example. Some comrades say that the average per capita output of steel in the U.S.A., the Soviet Union, Yugoslavia, and Romania is one-half to one ton. But we only have 30 some kilograms. Too low. We spent more than 3 billion U.S. dollars to import more than 8 million tons of steel products last year. This indicates that steel was scarce, and not abundant. These statements seem to make good sense. Let us analyze them in detail. At the end of 1977, the inventory of steel products was 12.6 million tons, higher than what was reasonable. Therefore, the 1978 plan required that 1.5 million tons of steel products from the inventory be used up. What happened? By the end of 1978, the inventory of steel products reached 15.5 million tons, an increase of 2.9 million tons. The actual consumption of steel products was 4.4 million tons less than what was planned, representing more than half of the imported steel products. Why did we send our steel products to the warehouses and import steel products at the same time? One of the reasons was a mismatch between variety, specifications, and needs. Why didn't we produce more steel products that met our needs? And why did we produce so many steel products that did not meet our needs? In addition to the small proportion of high-quality alloy steel, one important reason was that our past emphasis on "steel as the key link" resulted in a faster increase in our refining capacity than in our rolling capacity. Overseas, the rolling capacity always exceeds the refining capacity because the frequent changes of rollers to make the up to 10,000 to 20,000 varieties of steel products necessarily reduce the output of steel products. Because of our inadequate rolling capacity, we are forced to reduce the number of varieties and specifications in order to fulfill output targets. Very often we roll a lot of heavy, thick, and rough products regardless of needs. But we still receive awards because we have overfulfilled our refining and rolling tasks. What is regrettable is that we end up overstockpiling steel ingots and steel products in our warehouses while importing steel products that we really need.

My personal view is that last year's output increase of 7 million plus tons of steel is not necessarily a good thing. If we produced 2 million plus tons less of steel, and consequently 2 million plus tons less of steel products, we could have improved the quality of steel, increased its variety and specifications, shifted our inventory to production uses, and probably reduced our import of steel products. If we further used the fuels and power thus saved on light industry, we could have produced a lot of light industrial products. This year's market supply could have been eased somewhat. Our tight supply of fuels and electricity now is related to our heavy emphasis on steel. This year, the original plan called for an output of 34 million tons of steel. Later it was reduced to 32 million tons. But steel output in the first half year exceeded 17 million tons. And the annual output may well exceed 34 million tons. Inventory of steel products already exceeded 18 million tons at the end of June. It may well exceed 19 million tons at the end of the year. Compared with last year, we will have increased the inventory by 3 million plus tons, and idled 2 billion plus yuan more of circulating capital. What is the benefit of this kind of high speed to the country and to the people?

Another view thinks that steel products are indispensable for modernization. And the shortage of steel products is increasing. If we do not catch up, this shortage will get even worse. Then it will be too late to do anything about it. I am not sure there is a shortage of steel products. At least, it is not as serious as is indicated in the plan. First, if there is a shortage of steel products, why does inventory keep increasing at a fast rate? Second, why does the machine-building industry which is the largest consumer of steel products overfulfill its plan when many machine products are being overstocked? How can we explain the doubling of its output when steel products are allocated by the "three 80% system?"*4 Third, does the need for steel products tend to increase over time? Output of steel in the U.S.A. already exceeded 100 million tons in 1953. It has stayed at around this level since 1964. But industrial output increased substantially in this period. The reason was that substitutes for steel products emerged continually. Output of steel in the U.S.A. is lower than in the Soviet Union. But its gross national product far surpasses the Soviet Union's. Fourth, the need for steel is very flexible. It depends mainly on the size of capital construction. But the need for food grain is extremely inflexible because it is very difficult to reduce population and food consumption. In 1960, 18 million plus tons of steel was produced. But shortage of steel products was still very acute because the size of capital construction was too large. In 1962, steel output declined by more than 60% to 6 million plus tons. But because capital investment was reduced by more than 80%, there was no shortage of steel products. Shortage of steel products in these few years resulted primarily from overextension of capital construction. This year, capital investment is reduced by 20% (9 billion yuan). But the steel products have already been used up to manufacture machines and equipment which will again add to the inventory. At present, the inventory of machine and electrical products has reached 50 billion yuan. A shocking waste. If capitalist enterprises were run like this, they would have had to declare bankruptcy long ago. Therefore, I think the shortage of steel products is an artificial shortage. Our present steel output is the fifth highest in the world. It is less than West Germany (39 million tons), and higher than the U.K., France, and other countries (about 22 million tons). However, our industrial output is far below them. This problem deserves careful study.

Some comrades claim that the machine-building industry is also underfunded because we have to import many sets of machines and equipment. Rather than importing foreign equipment, we should expand investment in our machine-building industry to make the equipment ourselves. This reason does not hold water either. China has the third largest number of machine tools in the world, more than West Germany and Japan (of course, we are not as well-equipped in large, precision, and specialized machine tools as they are). China has several heavy machine-building plants whose size and number of equipment are rare even by world standards. Many of China's heavy industrial plants have huge repair workshops that can make their own machines and equipment. This is also rare in other countries. But even with all these machines and equipment, we still cannot produce advanced products. Many machines lay idle and many plants are producing large numbers of poor-quality products that are destined to be stockpiled in the warehouses for a long time. With so many machines and equipment laying idle, why should the state still be asked to finance more investment? In the past ten years or so, we imported several dozen sets of chemical fertilizers, synthetic fibers, petrochemicals, and other equipment. We did not seriously copy or improve on them. Now we still want to import more. This practice must be changed soon.

It must be pointed out that the machine-building departments and other industrial departments idle not only a large number of machines and equipment, but also a large number of engineering and technical personnel. The First Ministry of Machine-Building, Ministry of Metallurgy, and other industrial departments all have their own research institutes and design institutes. Some of these institutes often do not have any research or design tasks for long periods of time, thus idling thousands of engineering and technical personnel. After

the Party shifted its emphasis to the four modernizations, they were delighted by the prospects of doing some
useful work. But they are still laying idle. The reason
is that various industrial departments all want to import
machines and equipment from foreign countries. The First
Ministry of Machine-Building wants to make more accessory
equipment, or even some main engines. But there is so
much bickering between it and other departments over it
that there is no final decision. Without anything to
design, several thousands of research and design personnel can only wait around. We are short of engineering
and technical personnel for the four modernizations. But
we now have a lot of long-idled engineering and technical
personnel. Isn't this strange?

     Third, some comrades blame impractical theory for
throwing cold water on industrial production, leading to
lower growth. In the previous two years, industrial output grew at about 14%. This year, the planned growth
rate is only 8%. Next year, it will only be 6%. I think
the high growth rate in the previous two years did not
represent solid accomplishments. With higher output,
more profit had to be delivered to the higher levels.
But the products ended up being stockpiled in warehouses
with no customers. Last year, circulating capital
increased by 30 billion yuan. Many plants sold to
material resources departments low-quality products that
did not meet the needs of customers, or borrowed money
from banks to discharge their profit obligations to the
higher levels. Last year, inventory of steel products
and machine and electrical products in material resources
departments increased markedly. Commerce departments
also stockpiled a lot of slow-moving products. This
year, they are reducing their purchase of overstocked
products. Commerce departments not only are reducing
their purchase of overstocked products, but also are
reducing prices to get rid of part of their old stock and
report their losses. This way, the growth rate of
industrial output inevitably declines. In the first half
year, there should have been a budget surplus. But
instead there was a big deficit. It seems that conditions are indeed deteriorating. But if this year's
decline in the growth rate of industrial output results
only from a lower output of overstocked material resources, then it is a good thing, not a bad thing. The fast
growth rate of industrial output in the previous two
years contained a substantial portion of inflated growth,
which only added to an already overstocked inventory. It
was a case of dropsy. If this year a lower growth rate
of industrial output and a temporary budget deficit
result from a big reduction in our inventory of overstocked products, the health of our economy may recover
from this case of dropsy which has afflicted us for many

years. Then this year is in fact better than last year.
If we still encourage production of overstocked products
just to increase the growth rate, the situation will be
even worse.

To adjust, we must be prepared to reduce the growth
rate of industrial output temporarily. We cannot pretend
to be well-fed with the help of dropsy. When dropsy
deteriorates, not only will the growth rate decline, the
absolute level of output may also decline. This was the
case in 1961 and 1962. Once adjustment has been made and
health regained, the growth rate will naturally rise.
When output volume, output value, and budget revenues
dropped substantially in 1961, we did not fully appreciate the difficulties involved and were put on the
defensive. In 1962, we proposed a strategy of determined
retreat to consolidate our position before advancing.
Plants which produced low-quality products with high
input consumption and large losses were "closed, suspended, merged, redirected." The situation improved
right away. After good results were achieved after
adjustment, we again misjudged the soundness of our
situation. This happened when the 1963, 1964, and 1965
plans were formulated. Therefore, my view is that if
this year's adjustment is properly conducted, and our
dropsy is cured, then it does not matter whether the
growth rate of industrial output is below 8% or not.
What is frightening is the prospect that our dropsy will
not be cured, but instead will continue. Then not only
will the growth rate decline, the absolute figures may
also decline. Therefore, I think it may do us good to
review our experience and lessons from the three-year
"Great Leap Forward" and five-year adjustment.

Lastly, I want to talk about our goals in adjustment. I think there are short-term and long-term goals.
The short-term goal is to cure our dropsy. What we produce must meet the needs of the country and the people.
Capital construction should be retrenched to eliminate
all gaps so as to maximize economic returns. The proportional relations within heavy industry should be more
harmonious. People's living standards should show initial improvement. And the problem of labor employment
should be basically solved. It will not be easy to
accomplish all these goals in three years. If we do not
act determinedly with one heart, we may well end up
putting on a show and getting stuck with the same
illness. That is why I am sounding an alarm everywhere,
even though it may not please some people. The long-term
goal is to build up agriculture in a big way and build up
light industry next so that people's living standards can
be markedly improved. With the exception of food grain,
all unified purchase, quota purchase, and rationing
should be eliminated. Finally, even food grain should

be purchased at negotiated prices and supplied freely.
With agriculture and light industry well developed, not
only will there be plenty of commodities in the market
and people's living standard improved, there will also be
a big increase in exportable commodities. Fiscal revenues will also increase substantially. There will be
plenty of funds and foreign exchange for investment in
heavy industry. The whole national economy will come
alive. It will never be as tight as it is now. And
there will be plenty of breathing space. Of course, to
achieve these goals, we must not only adjust the national
economy with determination, but also do a good job in
reforming the economic management system. There may be a
greater resistance here than is encountered in adjustment. I cannot say anything more on this topic today.

     Today, I am giving you my personal views without any
reservations. There may be a lot of biases in them.
There are many comrades in the audience here who have
more experience than I. I hope you can suggest different
ideas. I must also point out that although I am a con-
sultant to the State Planning Commission, I cannot represent it. My views are entirely personal. It is a good
thing and not a bad thing to have different views. A
hundred schools can contend only if they have different
views. I hope there will also be a contending within the
Central Party School.

EDITOR'S NOTES

     *1. This refers to the socialist transformation of
agriculture, handicraft industry, and capitalist industry
and commerce.
     *2. The three red banners refer to the General
Line, the Great Leap Forward, and the People's Commune.
     *3. The moderization of agriculture, industry,
national defense, and science and technology.
     *4. Eighty percent of needs are approved; 80% of
these approved needs are accepted when order is placed;
and 80% of the accepted order are actually delivered.
See Xue Muqiao, "A Macroeconomic Approach to Improve
Economic Returns," People's Daily, June 2, 1981, p. 5.

3
Thirty Years
of Arduous Efforts
to Create an Economy

A TORTUOUS ADVANCE IN BUILDING SOCIALISM

China's First Five-Year Plan to build socialism was started in 1953. During the three-year recovery period, China's industrial and agricultural output grew very fast. Between 1949 and 1952, agricultural output grew by 48.5%, at an average annual rate of 14.1%. Industrial output grew by 145%, at an average annual rate of 34.8%. Among industrial output, light industrial output grew by an average annual rate of 29%. And heavy industrial output grew by an average annual rate of 48.8%. Of course, to a very large extent, these growth rates were only characteristic of the recovery period. They are impossible to achieve under normal circumstances. Because agriculture, light industry, and heavy industry grew at different rates, their proportions in the gross industrial and agricultural output[*1] had started to change. From 1949 to 1952, the relative share of agriculture declined from 70% to 58.5%, the share of light industry increased from 22% to 26.7%, and the share of heavy industry increased from 8% to 14.8%. The main reason why heavy industrial output increased so fast was because heavy industry suffered the most severe destruction in the war. After three years of recovery and development, its output exceeded the highest annual output in history. But its share in the gross industrial and agricultural output was still very small.

In the First Five-Year Plan, we learned from the Soviet Union by adopting the policy of priority development of heavy industry. With the aid from the Soviet Union, we started on 156 key projects (mainly in heavy

First published in Red Flag, 1979, No. 10.
This paper has three sections. Only the second section is translated here to avoid excessive duplication in content.--ed.

industry).   An initial foundation for socialist industrialization was laid. The achievements were remarkable.
But in order to construct so many heavy industries, a lot
of capital funds were needed. Under the existing conditions, this fund had to come from the peasants, as heavy
industry still could not provide any significant amount
of accumulation.   Light industry seemed to provide a
substantial   amount   of   accumulation.   But   its   raw
materials came mainly from agriculture. A large part of
its accumulation came from buying agricultural products
cheap and selling manufactured products (such as those of
the textile industry) dear.   It was transferred from
agriculture through exchange of unequal values.   More
importantly,   because   of   the   rapid   development   of
industrial production, urban population increased very
fast.   Supply of food grain, cotton fabrics, and subsidiary foodstuffs began to fall short. To ensure supply
to urban areas, the state had to resort to in-kind tax
and unified purchase of food grain and cotton.   Quota
purchase was later extended to meat, eggs, and other subsidiary foodstuffs. Quantitative rationing was adopted
for food grain, cotton fabrics, and even some subsidiary
foodstuffs.   In-kind tax, unified purchase, and quota
purchase limited consumption by peasants.   For several
years, excessive tax and purchase reduced consumption of
food grain to peasants and to some extent adversely
affected their production enthusiasm.
     In 1956, after extensive investigation by himself,
comrade Mao Zedong wrote the report "On the Ten Major
Relationships."   In   it,   he   pointed   out   that   heavy
industry should receive major emphasis in building
socialism. But agricultural and industrial development
must also be specially attended to. This report provided
a   correct   orientation   for   building   our   socialism.
Practice showed that a faster development of agriculture
and light industry not only could rapidly improve
people's standard of living, but also could provide a
large amount of accumulation to the state for accelerating the development of heavy industry. This way,
our road will widen as we proceed, and the superiority of
socialism will be fully exploited.
     In general, our First Five-Year Plan was basically
correct.   In these five years, our agricultural output
grew by 24.8%, at an average annual rate of 4.5%.   Industrial output grew by 28.6%, at an average annual rate
of 18%; of which, light industry grew at an annual rate
of 12.9%, and heavy industry grew at an annual rate of
25.4%.   In the gross industrial and agricultural output,
the share of agriculture declined from 58.5% to 43.5%;
the share of light industry rose from 26.2% to 29.2%; and
the share of heavy industry rose from 14.8% to 27.3% (the
above figures were based on constant 1952 prices).   The

156 major construction projects proceeded very smoothly with fairly good economic returns. What we should have done was to sum up experience and realize that a 24% average accumulation rate for five years was already too high, that the scale of heavy industry construction was already too large, and that the proportional relations between accumulation and consumption, and among agriculture, light industry, and heavy industry, must be suitably adjusted. In the First Session of the Eighth National Party Congress in 1956, comrade Zhou Enlai announced the proposed Second Five-Year Plan. This plan required that in 1962 output of food grain must reach 500 billion jin, but output of steel must reach only 10.5 million tons to 12 million tons. In five years, agriculture was to grow by 35% (24.8% in the First Five-Year Plan), and industry was to double (slightly more than 1.28 times that of the First Five-Year Plan). It now appears that this plan was correct. If it had been so implemented, greater achievements than those in the first five years could have resulted.

But, because we completed the socialist transformation of agriculture, handicraft industry, and capitalist industry and commerce ten years ahead of schedule in our First Five-Year Plan period, the Party was too complacent to be cautious. In the "Great Leap Forward" of 1958, steel output was to be doubled from 5.35 million tons in 1957 to 10.7 million tons, and output of food grain was to increase from 390 billion jin to 700 billion jin. Thus, objective laws of economic development were seriously violated. In that year, steel output actually reached only 8 million tons, and output of food grain reached only 400 billion jin. There was another wave of exaggeration fever in 1959. Steel output was to reach 18 million tons, and output of food grain was to reach 550 billion jin (August adjusted figure). Actual steel output reached 13 million plus tons and output of food grain and other agricultural products dropped substantially. In 1960, targets were raised even further. Actual steel output rose to 18 million plus tons and agricultural output continued to drop. In three years, the accumulation rate reached about 40%, resulting in serious imbalance in the proportional relations of the national economy and a marked drop in people's living standards. Practice told us that national economic planning must follow objective laws of economic development. If the proportional relations of the national economy were destroyed, it would it be impossible for heavy industry to develop at high speed; instead it would be forced to retreat.

In the winter of 1960, the Party Central Committee announced the policy of "adjustment, consolidation, enrichment, and improvement." The key to this policy was adjustment. The state was determined to lower output targets for heavy industrial products (especially steel and coal), reduce the size of investment substantially, and retrench capital construction by suspending many unfinished projects. The state also laid off about 20 million of the 25 million staff and workers recruited from the rural areas and returned them to the rural areas to strengthen the agricultural front. Because this policy was thoroughly implemented under the leadership of Premier Zhou, the national economy began to turn around in 1962. It fully recovered by 1965. During the three-year "Great Leap Forward" and five-year adjustment, the following changes took place in the proportional relations among agriculture, light industry, and heavy industry (at constant 1957 prices):

	1957	1960	1965
Agriculture	43.3%	20.1%	29.8%
Light industry	30.1%	26.6%	35.4%
Heavy industry	26.6%	53.3%	34.8%

At the end of the Second Five-Year Plan (1962), none of the departments of the national economy reached the targets of the proposed Second Five-Year Plan. After three more years of adjustment, steel output in 1965 reached the target specified in the proposal (12 million tons), and output of food grain recovered close to the 1958 level (400 billion jin) but still short of the target specified in the proposal. After this detour, in the eight years from 1958 to 1965, agriculture grew only by an average annual rate of 1.5%, and industry by an average annual rate of 8%, much lower than those in the First Five Year-Plan period. People's living standards recovered to the 1956 and 1957 level. But because the policy of adjustment, consolidation, enrichment, and improvement was thoroughly implemented, industrial and agricultural output continued to grow at a fairly high speed in 1966. The reason why economic work in the three-year recovery period, the First Five-Year Plan period, and the adjustment period between 1963 and 1966 was relatively successful was because we paid more attention to objective laws of economic development. It is not surprising that we still miss the pleasant memories of these years.

After 1966, Lin Biao and the "Gang of Four" abused the leadership power which they usurped during the "Cultural Revolution" to fan up a wholesale civil war. In 1967, agricultural output stagnated and industrial output dropped substantially. Steel output declined from 15 million plus tons in 1966 to 10 million tons. In 1968, output of food grain declined by 4%. Industrial output continued to drop, with steel output reduced to 9 million tons.   In 1969, Chairman Mao Zedong and Premier Zhou Enlai forbade large-scale armed conflicts. The political and economic orders began to recover, and industrial and agricultural output started to increase. In 1970, industrial and agricultural output increased substantially. Steel output rose to nearly 18 million tons and output of food grain exceeded 480 billion _jin_.   In the Third Five-Year Plan (1966 to 1970), the growth rates of industrial and agricultural output, although higher than those of the previous eight years, were markedly lower than those of the First Five-Year Plan period.

In the first few years of the Fourth Five-Year Plan (1971-1975), Premier Zhou Enlai proposed to criticize extreme Left thought.   Industrial and agricultural output developed relatively smoothly.   In 1973, steel output reached 25 million tons and output of food grain reached 530 billion _jin_.   In 1974, the "Gang of Four" used the campaign to "criticize Lin Biao and Confucius" to point their evil spear at Premier Zhou in an attempt to usurp the Party and seize power.   Once again, industrial and agricultural output suffered serious setbacks.   Steel output declined to 21 million tons.   In 1975, comrade Deng Xiaoping assisted Premier Zhou Enlai to thoroughly implement Chairman Mao Zedong's instruction relating to building up the economy.   In that year, industrial output rose by 15.1%, steel output recovered to 24 million tons, and agricultural output also increased over the previous year.   In these five years, the growth rate of agricultural output was about the same as in the previous five years.   Industrial output was slightly lower than that of the Third Five-Year Plan period.   In 1976, the "Gang of Four" launched a "counterattack on the Right deviationist attempt to reverse verdicts" in an all-out attempt to seize power. Once again, industrial and agricultural output suffered serious setbacks.   Steel output again declined to 21 million tons. Enterprises were poorly managed, resulting in huge losses.   The budget deficit reached 5 billion plus _yuan_. The whole national economy was on the brink of collapse.   The Party Central Committee as headed by comrade Hua Guofeng smashed the "Gang of Four" conspiracy to usurp the Party and seize power and saved the Party and the state from a crisis unprecedented since the founding of New China.

Although reductions in output during the "Cultural Revolution" were not as large as those suffered in the late 50's and early 60's, the resulting difficulties were more serious.   In the late 50's and early 60's, although there was greater hardship in people's livelihood, our leadership ranks at various levels of Party and government agencies were unified.   Under the leadership of the

Party and the government, the laboring people of the whole country advanced fearlessly so that the crisis was resolved in a short time. This time, prolonged sabotage by Lin Biao and the "Gang of Four" inflicted serious injuries on the Party's organization, thought, and style. The resulting factionalism and anarchism still exert their evil influence today. Even after three years of adjustment, management and labor discipline in many enterprises have yet to recover the status existing before the "Cultural Revolution." It is still necessary to make further adjustment.

In 1977 and 1978, our national economy began to turn for the better. In 1977, agricultural output did not increase, while industrial output rose by 14.3%. In 1978, because the Party's economic policies for the rural areas were enforced, agriculture still enjoyed a bumper harvest even in the face of very severe natural calamities. Agricultural output was 9% higher than for the previous year. Industrial output also grew by 13.5%. In 1978, steel output exceeded 30 million tons, and output of food grain reached 600 billion jin (300 million tons), both surpassing the highest records in history. It should be pointed out that the growth in these two years was recovery in nature. There are still great potentials for higher output in our industry and agriculture. If they are well managed, faster growth may be possible. Apart from chaotic management as mentioned earlier, our present obstacle to growth in industrial and agricultural output is proportional imbalance in the national economy. Many enterprises suspend or reduce production due to shortages of electricity, coal, steel products, timber, and cement. If the proportional relations are properly adjusted, it may still be possible for output to increase substantially.

In the past 30 years, although our socialist construction underwent several detours, the general achievements are still quite substantial. According to statistics from the State Statistical Bureau, from 1952 to 1978, industrial output grew by an annual rate of 11.2% and agricultural output grew by an annual rate of 3.2%. Although China's industrial output suffered several setbacks, its growth rate was still relatively high. But agricultural output grew more slowly. Particularly with respect to output of food grain, its annual growth rate of 2.4% was only slightly higher than the growth rate of the population (2%). In this period, we made many mistakes. Sometimes, our national economic planning paid attention only to increasing output, and little attention to improving people's living standards. It paid attention only to high speed, and little attention to proportions. Our accumulation rate was too high and capital construction was overextended. Not only were

people's living standards adversely affected, economic
returns from investment were also lowered. In production, we often blindly pursued output volume and output
value, resulting in poor quality, mismatches between
variety and specifications on the one hand and people's
needs on the other, and substantial losses. In the past
22 years, although industry grew at a respectable speed,
economic returns were very poor. And also because of
slow growth in agricultural output, people's living standards improved very little. These phenomena showed that
we did not do things according to basic economic laws of
socialism and the laws of planned and proportional development of the national economy at all. As a result, the
superiority of the socialist system could not be fully
exploited. We must seriously sum up experience so that
we can advance better in the future.

EDITOR'S NOTES

     *1. Gross output is gross of multiple countings in
value added. For a detailed explanation of the gross
output measure, see "Gross Output and Related Issues,"
in Sun Yefang, Some Theoretical Issues in Socialist Economics, ed. and trans. by K. K. Fung (Armonk, N.Y.:
M. E. Sharpe, Inc. 1982). The same applies to other
figures relating to relative shares in the gross output
in this and other papers.

4
Commune and Brigade Enterprises

I. BRIGHT PROSPECTS FOR COMMUNE AND
    BRIGADE ENTERPRISES

Commune and brigade enterprises are newly emerging
things that have developed quickly since 1970. In 1974,
80% of the communes and 60% of the brigades in the country had their own enterprises employing about 10 million
people, with an output of about 15 billion yuan.   In
1977, 93.6% of the communes and 76.6% of the brigades had
established enterprises.   These enterprises employed 23
million people, representing 7.7% of the rural labor
force, and produced an output worth 39 billion yuan,
amounting to about 50 yuan per capita agricultural population of the country. Development is very uneven over
the country, with suburban areas enjoying the fastest
growth. The average per capita agricultural population
output from commune and brigade enterprises in the suburban counties of Shanghai reached 304 yuan. The equiva-
lent figures were 180 yuan in the suburbs of Tianjin, 143
yuan in the suburbs of Beijing, and 103 yuan in Jiangsu
province. In Wuxi county, which has the highest average
per capita agricultural population output from commune
and brigade enterprises in the whole country, the figure
reached 383 yuan.   In ten provinces and autonomous
regions, namely, Guangxi, Shaanxi, Qinghai, Gansu,
Yunnan, Xinjiang, Sichuan, Anhui, Guizhou, and Xizang,
the per capita figure does not even reach 20 yuan. Commune and brigade enterprises developed very fast.   In
1977, the national output from state industry and agriculture was 12.6% higher than that of 1976. But commune
and brigade enterprises grew by 44.7%.
Development of commune and brigade enterprises provides immense impetus to agricultural production.   To
promote agricultural mechanization, most communes and

September 12, 1978.

many brigades established agricultural machine repair
plants to repair agricultural machines and manufacture
small agricultural machines, spare parts, accessories,
and small farm tools. Some communes even established
small chemical fertilizer plants and small agricultural
chemical plants. In many regions where commune and brigade enterprises enjoyed relatively fast growth, commune
and brigade enterprises accumulated a large amount of
capital funds for agricultural production. According to
statistics from the Ministry of Agriculture and Forestry,
in 1977 commune and brigade enterprises of the whole
country made a profit of 7.77 billion yuan after paying
to the state 2.2 billion yuan in taxes. The sum of the
two amounted to about 10 billion yuan. According to statistics from 11 provinces, municipalities, and autonomous
regions, communes and brigades used 13% of these profits
for farmland capital construction and 20% for buying agricultural machines; in addition, part of the profit was
used to aid poor teams. Based on these figures, about 3
billion yuan of the profits from commune and brigade
enterprises were used for farmland capital construction
and buying agricultural machines, representing 60% of the
state budget appropriations (5 billion yuan) to aid agriculture. In regions where commune and brigade industries
were relatively well developed, the funds in aid of agriculture from commune and brigade industries far exceeded
the state budget appropriations. For example, in Wuxi
county, commune and brigade enterprises accumulated 87
million yuan in 1977 (91 yuan per capita average of agricultural population). About half of this was used to aid
agriculture, with a per mu average investment of 40 to 50
yuan. This is one of the important reasons for Wuxi
county's rapid development in farmland capital construction and agricultural mechanization.
     Development of commune and brigade enterprises also
greatly improved peasants' livelihood. Wherever commune
and brigade enterprises are better developed, not only
does agricultural production develop faster, members'
incomes are higher. Although profits from commune and
brigade enterprises are not distributed to members, wages
for workers in commune and brigade enterprises are delivered to production teams to be recorded as workpoints
and shared with other members. In 1977, the average per
member distribution in Wuxi county was 103.8 yuan, of
which more than half came from wages delivered to production teams from commune and brigade enterprises. Although Wuxi county is a high-yield producing area in food
grain, its production costs increased a lot when it was
transformed into a three-crop system from a two-crop system. Output was increased without bringing in higher
income. The labor compensation received by peasants from
food grain production was only enough to pay for their

foodstuffs. If there were no commune and brigade industries, there would be great hardship in peasants' livelihood. Therefore, various regions all regard "aid
agriculture with industry" as an important policy for
developing agricultural production and improving
peasants' livelihood.

Development of commune and brigade enterprises
brought about marked changes in the income proportions of
the three-level ownership of the people's communes.
According to statistics from the State Statistical
Bureau, the income proportions of the three-level economy
of the rural people's communes were: 15.9% from the
commune and 16.1% from the brigade, representing a sum of
32% (30.5% according to statistics from the Ministry of
Agriculture and Forestry); and 68% from the production
team. The income proportions of the three-level economy
of Wuxi's people's communes were: 32.6% from the
commune and 31.5% from the brigade, representing a sum of
64.1%; and only 35.9% from the production team. Rapid
changes in the income proportions of the three-level
economy of the people's commune provide the favorable
material conditions for gradually increasing the level of
public ownership in the people's commune in the future.

Development of commune and brigade enterprises is
changing the economic structure of the people's commune
and gradually orienting its development towards a combination of industry and agriculture. According to statistics of the State Statistical Bureau, the 1977 output
from commune and brigade enterprises in the whole country
was 32.3 billion yuan, representing 8.3% of the national
gross industrial output. Output from commune industries
in Wuxi county already represents more than 60% of its
gross industrial and agricultural output and exceeds its
agricultural output. China has a lot of people, but
little cultivatable land. At present, rural population
still represents 87.8% of the total population in the
country. After agriculture is mechanized, it is not
possible to let a large number of rural population pour
into existing cities. We can only develop industries
where rural villages and market towns are situated and
transform rural people's communes into a socialist new
countryside where industry and agriculture are combined.

Even now, many comrades still underestimate the significance of developing commune and brigade enterprises.
Some comrades are afraid that the development of industries by communes and brigades may slacken leadership
over agriculture and affect agricultural production.
Facts show that wherever commune and brigade industries
are developing faster, agricultural production is developing faster. Development of commune and brigade
enterprises is at present an important method to aid
agricultural production. Some comrades think that it is

a mistake in direction when the growth rate of commune
and brigade industries far exceeds that of state industries. They do not realize that the proportional change
in the three-level economy of the people's communes can
create conditions for elevating the public ownership in
rural people's communes. Other comrades are afraid that
development of rural commune and brigade enterprises may
hinder the development of urban state industries. They
particularly oppose the spreading of production of some
products from urban industries to rural industries. It
should be pointed out that the old path of concentrating
industries in urban areas is no longer viable. Only by
spreading industries to rural areas and gradually indus-
trializing rural areas on the basis of combining industry
with agriculture can disparities between industry and
agriculture and between urban and rural areas be narrowed
and a steady advance be made towards the great communist
ideal.

II.   PROBLEMS IN DEVELOPMENT OF COMMUNE
AND BRIGADE ENTERPRISES

     Commune and brigade enterprises are newly emerging
things of recent years. Difficulties and errors are all
but unavoidable in their development process. We must
actively help them to overcome difficulties and guide
them towards the correct direction. At present, the
major problems are:
     First, uneven development, which is mainly concen-
trated in regions where industry is better developed.
Commune and brigade industries were first started to
serve agricultural mechanization. Agricultural machine
repair and manufacturing plants were established one
after another wherever conditions were favorable. Some
plants developed from this basis to go on serving big
industries. They accepted orders from big industries to
process materials. Therefore, the closer they were to
industrial regions, the faster they developed. The
average per capita output in the various provinces, municipalities, and autonomous regions that were mentioned
earlier fully illustrates these conditions. Development
is uneven in the same province. As far as I know, plants
are concentrated in the Suzhou and Changzhou areas in
Jiangsu province, and in Yantai and the Changwei district
in Shangdong province. The highest rate of development
in commune and brigade industries in Wuxi county is due
to its proximity to Shanghai city. Wuxi city is itself
an industrial city and has ready access to machines and
equipment. More importantly, there are a large number of
retired, elderly workers in this area. (In the past,
most of the machine workers in Shanghai came from Wuxi

city.) They are highly skilled. Moreover, their close
connections with the big plants in Shanghai, Wuxi city,
and other places make it easy for them "find their own
ways."   These conditions are absent in the interior
provinces.   The above-mentioned places are already quite
affluent to start with.   After commune and brigade
enterprises are developed, industrial and agricultural
production develops even faster, thus widening their
disparities with the interior provinces.   In order to
enable commune and brigade enterprises of various regions
to develop healthily, it is necessary to consider each
region's characteristics and develop a large variety of
commune and brigade enterprises to suit local conditions.   Unthinking imitation from other places simply
will not work.

Second, in order to enable commune and brigade
enterprises to bloom all over the country, it is necessary to seriously examine the policies formulated by
various Central ministries in the past.   In the past,
many policies did not help peasants to develop commune
and brigade enterprises.   Instead, they hindered the
development of commune and brigade enterprises.

Recently, I conducted an investigation in Anhui
province.   (Commune and brigade enterprises in Anhui
ranked third from the last in the country, with an
average output per capita agricultural population of less
than 13 yuan.) I saw that there were abundant resources
in the forms of bamboo, lumber, and native and special
products.   These offer great potentials for developing
commune and brigade enterprises.   In Jinzhai county, 20%
of the area is land and 70% is mountains.   But in the
past, this area also "took food grain as the key link"
and did not pay enough attention to developing commune
and brigade enterprises with the mountain resources.
At Hefei, I convened a conference on developing commune
and brigade enterprises with the mountain resources.
Eight units participated.   I discovered that most units
were only concerned with completing their own tasks and
paid very little attention to developing commune and brigade enterprises with mountain resources.   For example,
the forestry bureau established many "bamboo and lumber
inspection stations" to forbid or restrict exportation of
bamboo and lumber products in the name of "protecting the
bamboo and lumber resources of the mountains."   The
result was the rotting away of bamboo and trees in the
mountains.   Rural sidelines were further devastated by
the "Gang of Four."   They cut off commune and brigade
sidelines and peasant household sidelines as if they were
"capitalist tails." Fengyang county is a poor place which
depends on food grain resold to them by the state for
half the year and bought with bank loans.   Peasants use
sorghum straws to make brooms to supplement their income.

In the past, even this activity was considered as "capitalist tails." All the tools for making brooms were confiscated. If the pernicious influence of the "Gang of Four" is not eliminated, there is no way commune and brigade enterprises can be developed.

In river and lake regions, the marine resources can be used to develop commune and brigade enterprises. After agricultural cooperativization, many regions prohibited peasants from freely harvesting fish and shrimps. The former fishermen were transformed into peasants. The state and communes and brigades often did not organize specialized groups to harvest or raise marine products. Wuxi county is a well-known "land of fish and rice." In the past, large amounts of fish and shrimps were shipped to Shanghai everyday. Now it does not even have enough to satisfy local demand. In recent years, the fishing fleet in Lake Taihu is declining in number. It is said that because of shortages of timber and tung oil, it is very difficult to build and repair boats. There has been a big reduction in fishing boats and nets. Also, the increased number of transportation links not only led to waste of energy, but also spoilage of fish. In the past 20 years, market supply of mountain products and marine products has been declining. It is now in a sorry state compared with the pre-Liberation period. The reasons behind this situation deserve some careful study.

Newspaper reports on comrade Hua Guofeng's recent visit to Xinjiang to inquire into methods of developing animal husbandry and manufacturing based on livestock products also mentioned the need to develop commune enterprises. Our big pastures are all located in the frontier regions. If livestock are transported over long distances to the interior, they may suffer loss of weight or death. It seems that it is an urgent task to develop manufacturing in pasture regions (including pelting and leather tanning). Local processing of livestock products and marine products in the interior should also be encouraged to avoid long-distance transportation.

Third, an urgent problem that requires a solution in developing commune and brigade enterprises is to ensure supply of raw and processed materials and machines and equipment needed by them. Commune and brigade industries were started after 1970. In the past, the industrial ministries were only concerned with state industries. Therefore, there were no accounts for commune and brigade industries in the supply of raw and processed materials. Some cadres said: "Commune and brigade industries are illegitimate children. They cannot apply for residence and are not entitled to food grain coupons and cloth coupons." These were insurmountable obstacles. Small farm tools were originally produced by cooperative plants. At present, most of them are produced by commune and brigade industries. But the steel products needed to make small farm tools (2.5 kilograms per agricultural laborer) and allocated by the state are still under the control of the Second Bureau of Light Industry. In some areas, the steel is not allocated to commune and brigade industries; or the allocation is too small, resulting in forced shutdown of some small farm tool plants. Last year, the Center decided to put rural handicraft cooperatives under the jurisdiction of the commune administration. The Second Bureau of Light Industry transferred the cooperatives in some areas to a lower level. But it did not transfer the raw and processed materials downward. Similar situations occurred in other industries. The ultimate reason for these occurrences is a great shortage of raw and processed materials. Even the plants under the control of the Second Bureau of Light Industry do not have enough raw and processed materials. To solve this problem, Shangdong province included commune and brigade industries under the jurisdiction of the Second Bureau of Light Industry. But there are still endless disputes over the allocation of steel products. No easy solution is in sight.

Commune and brigade industrial and mining enterprises are all poorly equipped, leading to very low labor productivity. Many products have low quality and high costs, and their production needs to be gradually mechanized. But the original regulation specifies that these means of production can be allocated only to state plants and cooperative plants and not to commune and brigade plants. Therefore, many small coal pits, small mines, and small cement plants do not have enough steel drills and dynamite. Commune bureaus of enterprises hope that the state can establish a separate account for commune and brigade industries in the allocation of raw and processed materials. But conditions of commune and brigade enterprises in various regions are extremely complex. Allocation from above is unlikely to be satisfactory. Under present conditions, it seems that we can only manage by department and require that the needs for raw and processed materials by commune and brigade industries for planned products at various levels are included by various ministries and bureaus in the allocation plan just like other industries. The Ministry of Agriculture and Forestry wants to include the steel products needed for small farm tools in the plan to avoid supply interruptions, and is now discussing this with the relevant departments.

Fourth, another problem that requires urgent study is how to include output from commune and brigade industries in the state plan. The agricultural machine repair and manufacture plants that were widely established in communes contributed a lot to agricultural mechanization. But there was no unified planning, resulting in too many models and unstandardized products. Some products were made by everybody, resulting in small-scale production, high production costs, and low quality. Economic returns from agricultural mechanization were severely affected (the expenditure of dead labor[*1] greatly exceeding the saving of live labor). In the future, it is necessary to reorganize gradually according to the principle of coordination through specialization. The dragon-like method of Changzhou is perhaps the best method to adopt. In this method, the whole people ownership system is combined with the collective ownership system, with the whole people acting like the dragon head and the collective (communes and brigades) acting like the dragon body. Production is coordinated, with individual responsibility for profit or loss. This way, supply, production, and marketing can all be smoothly carried out according to the state plan.

In the past, most commune and brigade industries that served big industries of urban areas developed on their own without any outside assistance. For example, the commune and brigade industries of Wuxi county, because of their high technical know-how, not only serve the big industries in Wuxi city, but also accept orders from Shanghai, other provinces, and even several Central ministries. These coordinating relations are very unstable. To prevent sudden interruptions of work orders, it is necessary to send people out to scramble. Also, because there is very little planning, very often too many communes and brigades are making the same products. If their activities are not included in the state plan, it is difficult for them to develop healthily. But the problem of how to include production tasks for other provinces and Central ministries in the plan for Wuxi county is still unsolved. Wuxi county is concerned that once these activities are included in the plan, work orders from Shanghai may be assigned to commune and brigade industries in the suburbs of Shanghai, bringing disasters to the commune and brigade industries of Wuxi county.[*2] The downward transfer of products from plants in Wuxi county and city also takes some time to carry out. If the plants of Wuxi city and county do not expand their production or shift to production of advanced products, they will not be able to fulfill their own production and profit quotas once their original products are transferred to a lower level. It appears that the problem of adjusting and reorganizing commune and brigade industries (including some local industries) that were developed haphazardly in the past is extremely complex and requires serious study.

Fifth, corruption, waste, speculation, and manipulation occur in some areas where strict control has not been exercised over commune and brigade industries. They resort to gifts, wining and dining, and briberies to scramble for their own raw materials and market outlets. Since their needs for raw materials, fuels, marketing, and railroad transportation have not been included in the state plan, they have to grease someone's palms to get anywhere. Some field personnel take these opportunities to line their own pockets and corrupt many staff and workers. These phenomena were mainly caused by the interference and sabotage of the "Gang of Four." But their pernicious influence still remains.

The commune and brigade enterprises of some areas are not financially independent and are still eating from the free communal kitchen. In the Tangshan area, some commune and brigade plants give their workers only a meager subsidy instead of wages. Labor compensation comes from production teams according to their recorded workpoints. Income from enterprises is controlled by Party secretaries at the brigade, commune, and county levels. They are free to spend it to entertain guests, to buy gifts, and to construct non-production related buildings. One county spent 50,000 yuan from the profits of commune and brigade enterprises to construct an office building, using "sample" marble contributed by commune and brigade enterprises. Commune and brigade enterprises should be strictly required to establish economic accounting and financial management systems. Past illegitimate transfer of manpower, food grain, and financial resources from production teams to support extravagances of leadership cadres should be rectified. Serious infractions should be sanctioned by disciplinary measures.

Sixth, leadership relations over commune and brigade enterprises also deserve further study. It is a good idea for the Ministry of Agriculture and Forestry to establish a bureau of commune enterprises to lead commune and brigade enterprises. This way, commune and brigade enterprises can be better directed to aid agricultural production. But if the Ministry of Agriculture and Forestry does not take care of supply, production, and marketing, it is like having "a mother without milk." The problems faced by commune and brigade enterprises still cannot be solved. I suggest that the Center call upon relevant ministries and bureaus to support commune and brigade enterprises. The Second Bureau of Light Industry under the Ministry of Light Industry should also give better care to commune and brigade industries and fairly allocate raw and processed materials provided from above. Supply and marketing cooperatives should encourage communes and brigades to develop native and special products, and products that are processed from local resources, by purchasing and transporting them. China has a lot of mountainous regions and there are also more pastures than cultivated land. Commune and brigade enterprises have hardly been started in these regions. I hope supply and marketing cooperatives can assist them in this direction. The Ministry of Commerce has assigned production tasks of small commodities for daily use to commune and brigade industries in some regions. The Ministry of Foreign Trade has assigned production tasks of export commodities to commune and brigade industries. They have greatly contributed to the development of commune and brigade industries in some regions. Their experience should be summed up and extended in the future. The Ministry of Machine-Building Industry can disperse some products, spare parts, and accessories that are made with less sophisticated technology to commune and brigade industries in rural areas, and organize coordination through specialization with state industry as the leading force. The Ministry of Coal, Ministry of Chemical Engineering, Ministry of Metallurgy, and Ministry of Construction Materials should also be responsible for aiding the development of commune and brigade industries.

Because many commune and brigade enterprises need to be managed by department, multiple methods should be adopted to include their activities in the plan. One method is to let local bureaus of commune and brigade enterprises exercise unified control, and also take care of various supply, production, and marketing business. Another method is to manage them by industrial department, with the bureau of commune and brigade enterprises being responsible for coordinating various plans and making suitable adjustments. Planning commissions at various levels should also coordinate plans from various departments and resolve conflicts between local state industry and commune and brigade enterprises. They should particularly ensure production and supply of products supporting agriculture. No simple methods should be used to include commune and brigade enterprises in the state plan. We must allow them to find their own way. We can consider them included in plans if they register with the departments in charge. If planning departments want to run the whole show, many commune and brigade enterprises will be forced to shut down.

I did very little work on commune and brigade industries in the past. My ideas are therefore only preliminary ones and are offered to you comrades only as points of reference.

EDITOR'S NOTES

    *1. Dead labor is labor already embodied in some
material form, such as buildings, machines, raw
materials, fuels, etc.
    *2. Shanghai, although geographically close to Wuxi
county, is a municipality under the direct jurisdiction
of the Central government with the same status as a province. Wuxi county, on the other hand, is under the
jurisdiction of the Jiangsu province. If plans are formulated according to the administrative network, rather
than the economic network, existing economic ties between
Wuxi county and Shanghai will be disrupted.

5
Wages

HOW TO REFORM THE WAGE MANAGEMENT SYSTEM

The first problem in the wage system that needs to be solved is the above-mentioned problem of "iron rice bowls."[*1] If these "iron rice bowls" are not broken, it is impossible to thoroughly implement distribution according to labor. This is an ingrained problem that cannot be easily solved. In the past, comrade Liu Shaoqi advocated a two-tier system. Newly hired staff and workers were to be told that they could be fired, promoted, or demoted. And this system was to be extended to existing workers after a trial period. Regrettably, it was not adopted because it was criticized as revisionist.

The "Gang of Four" wanted to do away with distribution according to labor. Their attempt led to serious problems of egalitarianism. The activism of the laboring people was greatly discouraged. After the "Gang of Four" was smashed, newspapers and magazines made a big fanfare to publicize distribution according to labor. And piece rates and bonuses were revived. Now it is suggested that in the future labor compensation should be tied to enterprise performance. Namely, it will be determined not only by the quantity and quality of labor expended, but also by the economic returns achieved by labor. This way, all staff and workers will be concerned with the operation and management of enterprises. And the superiority of socialism can then be truly realized. We have done a great deal of publicity work, but many difficulties still exist in implementation. Many theorists think that resistance comes from leadership agencies and

A Talk to the National Forum on Wage System Reform, March 24, 1979.
This paper has three sections. Only the third section is translated here to avoid excessive duplication in content.--ed.

leading cadres. If only the latter's thinking can be
changed, then theory and practice of distribution
according to labor will coincide. Experience shows us
that theory and practice never did and never will coincide. At present, egalitarianism is part of our social
ethos. Even if our leaders' thinking can be changed, it
may be difficult to change the thinking of the masses.
How much of the bonuses given out last and this year
follow the principle of distribution according to labor?
We have bought nothing but egalitarianism with so much
money. "A three-foot thick freeze is not the result of
one day's cold weather." It seems that a great deal more
work needs to be done before this problem can be solved.

Egalitarian thought among China's laboring people
goes back a long time and has something to do with the
free supply system used in the Revolutionary War years.
In the 20 years of Revolutionary War, we used a free
supply system for our armed forces and cadres. Because
everybody fought bravely and worked hard, we won the
Revolutionary War. For several years after the whole
country was liberated, old cadres from the old liberated
areas were still under the free supply system. It was
gradually changed to a wage system, starting from 1953.
In 1958, Zhang Chunqiao claimed in a published paper that
the change to a wage system was a mistake and that the
free supply system should be revived. This led to a big
debate. During the "Cultural Revolution," several
proposals were made to revive the free supply system.
The free supply system was very useful during the Revolutionary War years. At that time, tight fiscal restraints
made the free supply system the only feasible system.
But it was used only for the armed forces and cadres. It
was never used broadly among the peasants. What they
used was something like the New Economic Policy advocated
by Lenin in 1921. That is, after the peasants delivered
their tax grain to the government, surplus grain could
be freely sold in the market. Therefore, the free supply
system did not affect the development of agricultural
production. In 1942, comrade Mao Zedong in his Financial
and Economic Problems proposed to change the free supply
system in public plants to a wage system or a bonus
system, for the free supply system was not conducive to
stimulating the production enthusiasm of the workers and
consequently to developing industrial production.

After the cities were liberated, the free supply
system was already unsuited to the living and working
conditions then. First, the needs from life and work had
been upgraded, especially among high-level leading cadres.
To help with their demanding work schedules, they needed
wristwatches, pens, and other similar necessities.
Second, the free supply system could not be easily extended to include the needs of family dependents. Since

the state could not standardize all distribution in kind,
it had to allow various agencies to adapt the system to
suit their own requirements. Uneven distribution of
hardship and joy thus resulted. A few leading cadres
indulged in extravagance and waste. Some were even
involved in corruption and theft (such as Liu Qingshan
and Zhang Zishan). In the 1952 "three anti" campaign in
agencies, the masses put up big-character posters to
expose "corruption" and "waste" of certain ministers who
used public funds to buy themselves wristwatches and to
make clothes for their parents and children. The free
supply system could no longer be continued and was
gradually changed to a wage system from 1953 on.

At that time, staff and workers in state enterprises, schools, hospitals, etc. were put under a wage
system right from the beginning when these institutions
were taken over. It was basically a system based on the
original standards, with minor adjustments. After 1953,
a unified wage system was adopted. The new wage standards established an eight-grade wage system which basically followed the principle of distribution according to
labor. There were too many grades among staff and
workers of agencies. Wage differences were too high.
But wages for high-level cadres were greatly reduced
compared with those in old China. Already, democratic
elements, highly educated people, and leading personnel
in enterprises felt that their compensations were too low
and wanted to get extra subsidies or receive "reservation
wages." Wages for Communist Party members were too high
and were reduced by 10% to 20% in three steps. Wage
adjustments in 1956 basically followed the principle of
distribution according to labor. There was no more
planned and general wage adjustment after that. Many
staff and workers were not promoted for 10 or even
20 years. Masters and apprentices received similar
wages. Problems of egalitarianism continued to worsen.

Another reason for wage egalitarianism is that China
is still poor. Only a low-wage system can be adopted.
Many low-wage staff and workers still face great difficulties in their livelihood. In the past 20 years,
industrial and agricultural output did not increase
steadily, but fluctuated frequently. Consequently, the
living standards of workers and peasants did not increase
markedly. For some people, they even deteriorated.
Therefore, promotions and bonuses could not be awarded
strictly according to labor. We must also take care of
hardship cases. When our labor compensation is so low
that some people cannot even be assured of minimum livelihood needs, egalitarianism cannot possibly be eliminated.

Another reason is that China was originally a
country with predominantly small producers. Among the

people, there has always been a streak of egalitarianism
characteristic of the petty bourgeoisie. It can also be
called agricultural socialism. Particularly in the
"Cultural Revolution" when "profit in command" and
"material incentives" were opposed, the principle of
material interests was thoroughly purged. In the heyday
of the "Gang of Four," several proposals to adjust wages
were rejected by them. From 1957 to 1977, average wages
not only did not increase, but fell slightly. At the
same time, labor productivity in some departments also
declined. "Three persons' food shared by five persons"
became "three persons' work shared by five persons."
Since workers were not "compensated according to labor,"
they "labored according to compensation." During this
period, people's thinking was totally confused by such
attitudes as "it is better to do less than to do more"
and "it is better to do nothing than to do less." Lin
Biao and the "Gang of Four" called for "politics in
command" without any principle of material interests. As
a result, people's socialist consciousness increasingly
retrogressed. It appears that we must now implement the
principle of material interests on the one hand and
strengthen socialist thought education on the other to
make people realize that individual interests must be
compatible with social interests and immediate interests
must be compatible with long-term interests. Only by
building up industrial and agricultural output can an
affluent life be provided to everybody.

Wages alone are not enough to really improve
people's livelihood. Equally important are market
supplies and livelihood service industries. Wages are
very high in some frontier regions. But people's real
living standards are very low. Nobody wants to go there.
Those who went want to come back. In these regions,
priority should be given to improving people's living
standards. Without decent living standards for the
people, we cannot begin to talk about modernization.
Everybody says China has too many people and too little
land. Livelihood problems are not easy to solve. But
many frontier regions have a lot of land and very few
people. Why are their living standards even worse? It
can be seen that natural conditions are not the only
factor. The key lies in the state construction policies.
Thus, we once again return to the above-mentioned problem of employment. If tens of millions of people all
want to crowd towards the densely populated maritime
provinces, it is difficult to make rational arrangements
and take all factors into consideration. The principle
of distribution according to labor may also be impossible
to realize.

With respect to the wage system, I also have doubt
about the feasibility of unified wage standards. In old

China, living standards varied a great deal among
regions. Even within a single region, wages varied.
After the new wage standards were put into effect, many
people received reservation wages. Unified wage standards were indeed applied to newly hired staff and
workers. But due to transfers among regions and
industries, a big plant could have several or a dozen
sets of wage standards while the whole country was supposed to have a unified set of wage standards.[*2] In
addition, there were various subsidies. The more unified
the system was supposed to be, the less unified it
became. In the past, small cities had low wage grades
not only because they had low prices, but also because
lower wages reduced disparities between workers in the
cities and peasants in their neighboring rural areas.
After the wage grades were elevated, disparities among
workers were reduced, but disparities between workers and
peasants increased. Conditions in rural commune
enterprises were just the opposite. To reduce disparities between workers and peasants, the workers "worked in
plants, but received their compensation in their own
teams." Very often, the masters came from poor teams
with low wages while their apprentices came from rich
teams with high wages. Conflicts between workers and
peasants were resolved at the expense of greater
conflicts among workers within a plant. At present,
disparities between workers and peasants are still very
great. Disparities among regions and among communes and
brigades are still widening. As soon as one problem is
solved, another problem arises. There is no way to
simultaneously solve all the problems. Therefore,
unified wage standards are necessary. But there is
really no way to unify wage standards. With many different sets of wage standards in one plant, how can the
principle of distribution according to labor be implemented? Can we allow plants to have more flexibility in
rationalizing wage standards within a single plant?
Provided that total wages are fixed, enterprises can then
decide on methods of awarding promotions and bonuses.

In order to control total wages, promotions and
bonuses are at present determined as a percentage of the
total number of staff and workers or total wages. This
method is in itself an example of egalitarianism. It
cannot possibly reward the advanced. Plants with many
staff and workers and low labor productivity may have
more promotions and bonuses. Promotions and bonuses
should have been determined by regions or industries,
with a higher percentage for advanced plants and a lower
percentage for backward plants. But regions and industries are all afraid of disputes. They prefer to pass
this source of conflicts all the way down. Many big
plants even applied the same percentage all the way down

to workshops, teams, and groups. Egalitarianism is thus
inevitable. If egalitarian distribution is not done away
with, bonuses will not appreciably improve labor productivity.

I have done very little work on labor wages and know
very little about them. Therefore, my talk today raises
more questions than it gives answers. The problems I
have raised are big and difficult. But these problems
must be solved. Although we may not be able to solve
them now, we must think about and discuss them. We cannot postpone their solutions forever. The longer we
postpone, the harder they are to solve. If my talk today
can help you all to take a broader and longer view of
things, I think I have achieved my objective.

EDITOR'S NOTES

*1.   "Iron rice bowls" refer to jobs in state
enterprises, agencies and institutions with guaranteed
security against dismissal and demotion.
*2.   The 1953 national wage scales divided the
country into ten wage zones, each separated by a 3% dif-
ference in pay. Small towns were assigned to the lower
wage zones, and large cities and frontier regions to the
higher wage zones. Also, within each wage zone, wages
were higher in industry than in commerce, in heavy
industry than in light industry, and in light industry
than in the handicrafts. Staff and workers who were
transferred from a higher wage zone (and/or industry) to
a lower wage zone (and/or industry) were allowed to carry
their old wage scales with them so as not to reduce their
accustomed living standards. For further details, see
Xue Muqiao, China's Socialist Economy (Beijing: Foreign
Languages Press, 1981), pp. 84-86.

6
Comments on Employment in Cities and Towns

China is a large country, with 970 million people. With so many people and a weak economic foundation, labor employment is an extremely difficult problem to solve. Because of slow development of production and other reasons, 7 million plus laborers are waiting to be allocated this year. If this problem is not solved, the country's stability and solidarity will be greatly affected.

This year, some places experimented with voluntary early retirement to open up vacancies for children of early retirees. As a result, many older skilled staff and workers retired to be replaced by a batch of unskilled youths. Many of these youths were originally students still attending school, and some worked in rural areas. Very few young urban job seekers actually found jobs. Many older staff and workers were recruited by other units after their retirement. The number of staff and workers increased, but the number of job seekers has not decreased.

In the past, the labor wage system was too rigidly controlled. Employment of staff and workers was all centrally allocated by labor departments. Enterprises did not have autonomy in personnel matters. Staff and workers had no right to choose their jobs. If this problem is not solved, "from each according to his ability" simply becomes empty talk. More importantly, the state must strictly control the total number of newly created jobs for staff and workers, as the number of job seekers is several times the number of state job vacancies. Since the state cannot offer to every young job seeker an "iron rice bowl," and it also does not permit them to organize on their own in some collective form to perform urgently needed labor, the number of job seekers gets larger all the time.

First published in Beijing Daily, July 18, 1979.

China does not lack experience in solving labor
employment. When the country was first completely liberated, there were 3 to 4 million unemployed people in
cities, roughly equal to the number of staff and workers
in public and private enterprises. We adopted two
measures. One was "production through self-help." Unemployed people were encouraged to find their own ways,
with the state helping to solve problems encountered in
production. The other was "public service employment,"
with the state sponsoring certain public projects at low
wages. Within a year or two, the problem of unemployment
was basically solved. In the First Five-Year Plan
period, we were still suffering from unemployment. The
solution was to "share three persons' food with five
persons" by lowering wages and increasing employment.
But it became "five persons sharing three persons' work,"
leading to low labor productivity in plants and low work
efficiency in offices. Now it is time we made changes.

In the beginning of the 50's, job seekers could
still find their own ways. After whole trades were
changed into joint state-private ownership, especially
after joint state-private commerce (in the beginning,
much joint state-private commerce was financially independent) was elevated to state commerce, and handicraft
cooperatives were elevated to cooperative plants, all
staff and workers were centrally allocated by labor departments. The original handicraftsmen and small mer-
chants operated within a dense network and displayed a
great variety both in product and mode of operation. At
present, the density of the network and the variety of
product is greatly reduced. Many native and special
products with unique characteristics have disappeared.
In the past, there were many shops in the Dongan market
of Beijing, each with their unique characters. Under
unified operation, the Dongan market has now been transformed into a second department store with none of its
original unique characters. In the First Session of the
Eighth National Party Congress in 1956, comrade Chen Yun
suggested in his speech that joint state-private shops
and cooperatives should not be merged without any limit,
and that product variety and operational flexibility must
be preserved. But, after 1958, financially independent
joint state-private shops and handicraft cooperatives
were all but eliminated. Many native and special products were chronically short. With no one to produce and
to operate, the service industry was decimated. On the
one hand, a lot of work urgently needed by society is not
performed by anybody. On the other hand, many laborers
cannot find suitable work. It is not a question of not
having any work to do, rather they must wait for central
allocation by the state. And there are only a limited
number of vacancies in enterprises under whole people

ownership in urban areas. Consequently, the ranks of young job seekers continue to swell.

Recently, comrade Hua Guofeng announced in his report on government work to the Second Session of the Fifth National People's Congress that three years will be spent on adjusting, reforming, reorganizing, and improving the national economy. He also announced ten current tasks to develop the national economy. The ninth task relates to the current critical problem of labor employment. If this problem is not solved, not only will a large amount of labor be wasted, stability and solidarity will also be affected. Also, if we do not solve this problem resolutely now, the burden will get even heavier in the future. (Our present labor productivity in big plants is five to ten times lower than that in developed capitalist countries.) If we want to raise labor productivity of workers in the process of modernizing our national economy, we will find that there are far too many laborers in our enterprises. Many agency offices are similarly overstaffed and must be streamlined to improve work efficiency. There are now 300 million laborers in agriculture. If it is mechanized, only several ten million people will be needed. The rest of the people must find alternative jobs, in addition to jobs opened up by extending the depth and breadth of agricultural production. We must anticipate these problems and plan for them accordingly. At present, our cities cannot support all these people. And since peasants cannot even maintain their own livelihood, there are also limited opportunities in rural areas. The ultimate solution to labor employment is still to develop production and open up employment opportunities in a big way. One important way to open up employment opportunities is to change the labor management system.

At present, all young job seekers are centrally assigned jobs by labor departments. This system can no longer be continued. If we rely on the state to give each person an "iron rice bowl," there will be a shortage of "bowls." Also those who get them cannot be fired or demoted. In the modernization process, there is conflict between improving labor productivity and handling labor employment. On the one hand, when enterprises adopt economic accounting, they want to lay off some unneeded and incompetent staff and workers for labor departments to reassign. On the other hand, in order to place young job seekers, labor departments want enterprises to employ children of their own staff and workers. Both sides have difficulties. It is only natural that each side tries to shift the problem to the other side. To realize modernization, the former request is rational and the latter request is irrational. Labor departments need to think of other ways. There is only one way.

What cannot be taken care of by them should be let go. We should allow young job seekers to organize production in some form. Not only should we not prohibit them, we should also help them, organize them, and lead them. At present, there are numerous employment opportunities in urban areas. The question is whether we let the job seekers find their own ways. One leading cadre in the Beijing municipal committee told me that there were so many so-called "capitalist loopholes" in Beijing that it was almost impossible to close them. It was very easy for a peasant to go into the city to make 2 to 3 yuan a day doing odd jobs. In the past, the municipal committee considered these peasants "capitalist roaders" and sent them right back to where they came from. But many agencies, plants, and shops in turn got them back. Migration of peasants to urban areas should, of course, be controlled. Can we open up these "loopholes" to urban young job seekers?

Some comrades say that only peasants are interested in exploiting these "loopholes." Urban young job seekers are not similarly interested. They do not accept placements in service industries. This is a result of trying to fit a round peg into a square hole. If educated youths with specialized knowledge are assigned to work in service industries, it is natural that some of them may not want to do it. I heard that one service industry received several times as many applications as there were vacancies when it tried to recruit several dozen staff and workers. If we can change "arranged marriages" into "free loves," this problem can be easily solved. This way, the recruiting enterprises can select the best available candidates. And young applicants can also satisfy their desires. In the past, neither side was allowed to exercise free choice. Enterprises could not get the people they wanted, but had to accept those they did not want. Young job seekers were not allowed to do the jobs they wanted, but had to accept what they did not want. How can such a labor allocation system be maintained?

If labor departments want to control the total amount of wages for staff and workers, they must not concentrate only on state enterprises and state agencies, etc. Labor departments' job allocations create state staff and workers with "iron rice bowls" who cannot be fired, regardless of performance. If job seekers are allowed to find their own jobs by banding into financially independent cooperatives or small cooperative groups, then the state does not have to pay their wages. Also, with higher labor activism and better service attitude, one person can do the work of several persons. Their labor income will not be less than that of a third- or fourth-grade worker. Why should these things be

prohibited?   Such arrangements can not only solve the
employment problem of a large number of people, but also
bring convenience to the life of urban residents.   Indeed, two birds can be killed with one stone.
     There is much work that needs to be done in urban
areas. For example, transportation. When the state cannot even do a good job in handling long-distance transportation, it certainly does not have enough resources to
take care of intra-city short-distance transportation.
Our present reliance on peasants to drive tractors to
make deliveries into cities presents a great deal of
inconvenience.   If the state runs transportation companies, they in turn become "iron rice bowls" and
inaccessible to users.   Before Liberation, Shanghai's
Xiangsheng rental car company, household moving companies, etc. were well run, providing much convenience to
residents. In the 50's, it was still possible to hire
wooden carts to move household effects. Now they cannot
even be found anymore. In the past, there were people in
stations and airports helping move luggage. Now they can
no longer be found. One foreign princess was prepared to
offer U.S. $10 for someone to carry one piece of luggage.
She could not find anyone to do it and ended up carrying
her luggage for the first time.   Incidentally, in the
past, many stations had people selling special native
products, such as roast chickens of Dezhou and Fuliji,
spare ribs of Wuxi, soy sauce pig feet of Fengjing, etc.
Several years ago, these businesses were completely eliminated. They have been revived to some extent now. But
they are still too few in number. Before Liberation,
licenses were required to peddle goods in stations for
one yuan a day. Not only did the peddlers make a lot of
money, but the stations also made a lot of money. Not
only were passengers spared having to join the big crowds
in dining cars so often, but they could buy various special native products as gifts for their relatives and
friends. Why can't such businesses with multiple benefits be conducted?
     There are also severe labor shortages in building
construction in urban areas. Can job seekers be allowed
to organize some construction troops with collective
ownership? I heard that recently some retired construction workers organized on their own a contractor team.
They did high-quality work in record time and enjoyed
great popularity. The authorities ordered them to dis-
band because they were receiving retirement benefits.
But this order was ineffective because many agencies,
plants, and schools competed for their services. Can we
allow these elderly workers to lead some youths in organizing legal contractor teams to solve problems of
housing construction and repair? I must mention another
problem in passing here. At present, it is difficult to

get illnesses treated.   Some people want to see retired
doctors.   But the state does not allow elderly doctors on
retirement benefits to see patients and prescribe medi-
cines.   We all know that many retired doctors are more
experienced than the interns in big hospitals.   Why must
their talents be wasted?

We all know that labor shortages exist in restaurants, repair shops, and other service businesses and
lead to a lot of wasted time among staff and workers as a
result.   Recently, Beijing has plans to open up more
restaurants and serve midnight snacks in several big
restaurants.   But there are more service people than
customers in these midnight snack places.   Why?   Residents can spend 0.1 yuan for a bowl of wonton or red bean
soup served from curbside stands.   There is no need to go
to big restaurants.   Can we encourage some people to set
up small eating places on sidewalks of streets and lanes?
There are problems in repair businesses, too.   Regular
shops take a week to repair a pair of shoes.   Small
stands can fix them right away.   You cannot find anybody
to mend clothes or to repair broken tables and chairs.
Why can't we allow people to set up small shops and
stands to provide these services?   We should learn from
Shanghai's experience in urban repair businesses.
Another business that has been overlooked for many years
is laundry.   Before Liberation, there was a laundry in
every neighborhood in many big and medium cities.   Some
people collected laundry from colleges and high schools
to wash every day.   Staff and workers of agencies usually
did not have to wash their own laundry.   At present,
doing laundry is second only to preparing meals in time
and efforts spent.   If the laundry business is revived,
with some washing machines, then staff, workers, and students will have more time to study or rest.   They need
not work harder on Sundays than on weekdays.

The above-mentioned are all businesses that need to
be established or increased.   In the past, some people
regarded them as "capitalist loopholes" that could not be
effectively stopped.   Now these loopholes need to be enlarged into large doors to develop enterprises with collective ownership.   The constitution allows "individual
labor that is within the law and does not exploit other
people."   This stipulation should also be implemented.
This way, the urban employment problem can be solved.
Recently, there were some successful pilot projects in
the Chongwen district of Beijing.   Some people worry that
errors in line may be committed if the income of some
people working in financially independent, collectively
owned businesses in urban areas is more than that of a
fifth- or sixth-grade worker.   They hope that the
theorists can write a few more papers to show that
collectively owned businesses in urban areas are not an

example of taking the capitalist road.   My above-
mentioned examples all involved hand labor.   So far as
hand labor is concerned, I think collective ownership may
be superior to whole people ownership.   Production
relations must be appropriate for the nature of productive forces.   To regard whole people ownership as always
(such as under the condition of hand labor) superior to
collective ownership is simply not Marxism.   At present,
not only must collective ownership be further encouraged
in urban areas, individual labor (such as mobile knife
sharpening and shoe repair services) must also not be
eliminated altogether.   These will not only expand
employment opportunities, but also provide convenience to
residents.   If we are firm in enforcing the rule that
people are only allowed to earn their own living and not
allowed to exploit hired labor, there will not be any
emergence of new exploiting elements.

7
Price Adjustment and Reform of the Price Control System

I. EVOLUTION OF THE PRICE PROBLEM

China's price problem underwent a complex evolution in the past 30 years. In February 1950, a decisive victory was won in the battle to stabilize market prices, with the state firmly in control. Following this, the state began to set prices for major industrial and agricultural products. But because of the co-existence of several economic components, the state had to correctly follow the law of value and the law of surplus value in setting prices. When the state placed orders with capitalist industries, it had to not only accurately calculate costs, but also allow a reasonable profit to the capitalists. When the state purchased agricultural products from peasants, it had to not only generate a reasonable labor return to peasants, but also regulate the output of various agricultural products by adjusting prices. We did a good job in combining plan regulation with market regulation until the socialist transformation of ownership in means of production was completed. During the three-year recovery period, market regulation predominated. But state planning gradually strengthened its guiding role. In the First Five-Year Plan, with the development of the socialist state economy, the emphasis was gradually shifted to plan regulation. But since the capitalist economy and the individual economy still existed widely, market regulation continued to play an important role. Therefore, state prices were basically in line with the law of value. Product prices constantly changed with changes in production costs and supply-demand conditions. At that time, the state's price policy was mainly to stabilize prices. Apart from reducing the price differentials between industrial and

---

July 5, 1980.

63

agricultural products, the question of price adjustment was not yet raised.

After the socialist transformation was completed, the state adopted the method of unified revenues and unified expenditures[*1] towards state industry. Because enterprises did not need to worry about their profit or loss, they were not concerned about whether prices were high or low. The state adopted the methods of in-kind tax, unified purchase, and quota purchase towards major agricultural products. With "plan coming first, and prices coming second," prices increasingly deviated from values. Although the state raised the purchase prices for agricultural products many times, and adjusted prices for industrial products to some extent, price adjustment lagged far behind changes in objective conditions. In general, because of limitations imposed by natural conditions, costs for agricultural and mining products seldom decline with higher output. On the contrary, they may even rise. On the other hand, costs for manufactured products decline with higher output. As these trends continue, profit for the former products will be very low or negative, while profit for the latter products will be very high. Prices for both types of products deviate more and more from their values (the former lower than values, the latter higher than values). Reasonable adjustment is therefore necessary.

In the three-year "Great Leap Forward," the national economy suffered from a proportional imbalance. As a result, agricultural output dropped. With a rapid growth of money, prices shot up. In 1962, when the National Price Commission was just established, it was determined to stabilize prices to control inflation. It put forth the policy of stabilization first and adjustment second. In the next two to three years, prices were basically stable, with some declines. Price adjustment was thus elevated to a primary position. A five-year plan to adjust prices was announced in 1965 and 1966. The policy was to gradually raise prices for agricultural products and some mining products. There were to be rises and falls in prices for light industrial products, with no overall upward or downward movements. Prices for some heavy industrial products (machines and chemicals) were to be gradually lowered. No sooner was the plan implemented than the "Cultural Revolution" started. For fear of disrupting the market, prices were temporarily frozen. In the next 12 years, prices were basically unchanged. The deviation of prices from values continued to worsen. As a result, agriculture, mining, and some raw materials industries were often unable to fulfill their production plans, while manufacturing industry, especially machine-building industry, overfulfilled their plans. Of course, unreasonable prices were not the major reason for the proportional imbalance in the national economy that was gradually formed over ten years. But it was one important reason.

Looking back, we now realize that the direction of the five-year price adjustment plan put forth in 1965 was correct. But it could not have thoroughly solved the price problem. First, the degree of price adjustment was too small, averaging only 1.2 billion yuan a year. This amount could at best only prevent the price differentials between agricultural products and industrial products from widening. It could not rapidly realize exchange of equal values between industrial and agricultural products or among industrial products. Second, there are hundreds of thousands of varieties of industrial and agricultural products with up to one million different prices. If market regulation is not used, the price departments alone will surely be unable to do a good regulating job. But if market regulation is to be used, the problem of reforming the whole economic management system must be faced. Moreover, even this half-hearted five-year plan to adjust prices was delayed for more than ten years. The situation has deteriorated so much that there are almost insurmountable obstacles to paying back these ten-year-old debts. If there are no determined and decisive measures, it will be very difficult to put our socialist economy back on the right track.

II. NEW PROBLEMS IN ADJUSTMENT AND REFORM

The year before last, the Third Plenary Session of the Party's Eleventh Central Committee shifted the emphasis of Party work to a new long march towards socialist modernization. In view of the present conditions, the first battle is to adjust, reform, reorganize, and improve. Starting from last year, we raised the purchase prices of agricultural products substantially. We continued to increase wages of staff and workers and resumed payment of bonuses. A 20-year debt to the people's livelihood was beginning to be repaid. At the same time, we are determined to reduce investment in capital construction, and change the unreasonable proportional relation between accumulation to consumption. Of course, it is not possible to completely repay a 20-year-old debt to the people's livelihood in three to five years. Last year's measures to improve workers', especially peasants', living standards greatly increased the production enthusiasm of the industrial and agricultural laborers. The results were truly remarkable. But the growth rate of people's income greatly exceeded the growth rate of output. This was inevitable if a 20-year debt was to be repaid. If we had been determined to reduce investment in capital construction, it might have been possible to maintain a budgetary and credit balance. The problem was that we overfulfilled our planned increase of the consumption fund and underfilled our planned reduction of the accumulation fund, leading to a budgetary and credit imbalance. This newly created social purchasing power destabilized prices in the market. To counter this problem, the Center was forced to resolutely stabilize prices, creating difficulties for the planned adjustment of prices.

While adjusting the national economic proportions, we started to implement reform of the economic management system. We combined plan regulation with market regulation by fully exploiting the regulating functions of the market under the direction of the plan. Market regulation is in fact regulation through the use of the law of value. Under the abnormal condition when prices deviate from values, current prices conflict with market regulation. We are thus forced to accelerate price adjustment. Our practical experience with institutional reform in the past one year or so has shown that if prices are not adjusted, many unresolvable problems will be encountered in institutional reform. For example:

1. When we expand enterprise autonomy, profit retention is used to encourage enterprises to increase output and practice economy and improve their activism in operation and management. This is undoubtedly a very good method. But as the prices of many products deviate substantially from their values, the size of enterprise profit does not depend mainly on operation and management, but rather on prices. Because prices are higher than values for products from some enterprises and lower than values for products from other enterprises, profit retention resulted in extremely uneven distribution of hardship and joy among enterprises. We should first adjust prices before we implement profit retention. But price adjustment is a big job and must be postponed. In order to reduce uneven distribution of hardship and joy, the proportion of retained profit is tied to the size of enterprise profit. But once this method is adopted, it creates obstacles to later price adjustment. If prices are raised, enterprises get more profit. That makes the fiscal departments unhappy. If prices are lowered, enterprises get less profit. That makes them unhappy. To change prices, the proportions of retained profit must then be changed, leading to many disputes.

2. In the past, many products were subject to
    unified purchase and guaranteed marketing.*2
    The great wall separating producing units and
    market needs led to chronic overstocking of many
    products and chronic shortages of many other
    products. Economic returns from production were
    greatly reduced as a result. Last year, market
    regulation was adopted for many products. Com-
    merce departments   purchased   selectively
    according to market needs. And what was not
    selectively purchased could be sold indepen-
    dently by plants. This way, what products are
    abundant or scarce began to be revealed. Indus-
    trial and commerce departments all must adjust
    production, purchase, and marketing according to
    market needs. But many abundant products com-
    mand high prices and large profits. Their out-
    put still cannot be reduced. Many scarce
    products command low prices and small profits.
    Nobody is willing to produce them. To adopt
    market regulation, we have to follow the law of
    value. Prices for abundant products should be
    allowed to fall, and prices for scarce products
    should be allowed to rise. If price departments
    do not actively make adjustment, and do not
    allow the law of value to assist us to make
    adjustment, great obstacles will be created for
    adjusting the proportional relations among
    departments of the national economy. This phe-
    nomenon is even more serious in the allocation
    of producer goods because of overly strict
    control.
3. Since market regulation was started, some plan
    prices have been suspended. For example, in
    order to organize coordination through speciali-
    zation in the machine-building industrial de-
    partments, profits among enterprises have to be
    adjusted. Coordination prices are set to
    supplant plan prices within and among some
    regions. Some coordination prices are higher
    than plan prices, others are lower. Apparently,
    coordination prices are more in line with the
    law of value than plan prices. Negotiated
    buying and selling prices are used to market-
    allocate producer goods. Some negotiated prices
    are markedly higher than plan prices. But there
    is nothing you can do about it. Only by raising
    plan prices and rewarding higher output (such as
    some minor steel products) will negotiated
    prices come down. For some chronically over-
    stocked products, material resources departments
    should not only allow unrestricted supply, but

also sell them at a discount. Or producing
units will not reduce output on their own. In
some big cities, markets for agricultural and
sideline products have recently opened, greatly
increasing the supply of products. Some products are purchased and marketed by negotiation
through supply and marketing cooperatives and
warehouses. Their prices are inevitably higher
than state prices. The opening of urban markets
this time is different from the three-year hardship period. At that time, fall in agricultural
output led to market prices many times higher
than plan prices. At present, market prices are
only slightly higher than plan prices (in some
areas, prices for food grain are even lower than
the incentive prices. In some areas, prices for
meat and eggs are lower than plan prices,
forcing state commerce to reduce prices to
increase sales). It is to be expected that such
negotiated transactions inevitably lead to some
speculation and manipulation. Management must
therefore be strengthened. But we should not
impose strict control. Too strict a control
will not be conducive to developing production
and improving people's living standards.

In short, once reform of the economic management
system is started, especially after market regulation
is adopted, the existing deviation of prices from values
cannot be maintained for long. Therefore, how to handle
the relation between price stability and price adjustment
once again becomes an item of the agenda in price work.
We must quickly formulate a series of concrete policies
to ensure that, provided prices for major livelihood
means are basically stable, prices for other products,
especially producer goods, can be adjusted upwards or
downwards to resolve the above-mentioned conflicts.
This time, price adjustment should not be handled exclu-
sively by price departments. Practice shows that this is
an impossible task for them to do. If we are going to
use market regulation, we must be good at using the law
of value to make prices of products gradually approach
their values. Therefore, in adjusting prices, price
departments should not concentrate on calculations, but
must seriously study problems relating to goals and policies. They must specially study how to use the law of
value so that our market regulation can facilitate
balance between supply and demand, and not aggravate
imbalance.

III. TENTATIVE PROPOSALS FOR PRICE ADJUSTMENT

    Many comrades think that there is conflict between
price stability and price adjustment. If prices are
adjusted upwards and downwards, the overall direction may
be more upward than downward adjustments. And it is felt
that price stability is very difficult to maintain. The
actual conditions are quite different. Fluctuations in
prices depend mainly on production development, and
especially the balance between money supply and social
demand for money; that is to say, the balance between
social purchasing power and social supply of commodities.
In our First Five-Year Plan period, although the state
still could not exercise strict planned management
because of the co-existence of several economic components, prices were basically stable because we carefully controlled money supply. In the Second Five-Year
Plan period, the state's planned management of prices was
greatly strengthened because the socialist transformation
was completed. But because agricultural output started
to decline in 1959, and money supply increased by 1.4
times between 1957 and 1961, prices in farmers' markets
shot up. Prices for minor commodities over which the
state did not exercise complete control also rose. To
protect people's livelihood, the state resolutely stabilized prices for 18 categories of major consumer goods.
But it also had to sell some high-priced commodities to
withdraw some money from circulation. From 1961 to 1964,
we withdrew 4 to 5 billion yuan of currency from circulation. And with agricultural output starting to rise
from 1962 on, prices in farmers' markets fell. There was
no demand for high-priced commodities anymore. Their
prices gradually fell back to their normal level.
Practice shows that provided that output rises, especially when money supply is not excessive (this requires
that budgetary and credit balances be maintained), prices
can be basically stabilized.
    It must also be pointed out that prices that deviate
from the law of value cannot really be stabilized. From
1961 to 1962, we tried very hard to stabilize prices.
But because of excessive money supply, only plan prices
could be stabilized. The rest of the money was forced
onto the farmers' markets. When money supply doubled,
prices in farmers' markets had to increase from three to
four times to five to six times. Price increases in
farmers' markets boost peasants' incomes. But they could
not withdraw money from circulation for the state.
Therefore, the state had to sell high-priced commodities
the prices of which were two to three times higher than
plan prices. This showed that the law of value still

exerted its regulating functions.   Not until after the
money supply was returned to normalcy were prices really
stabilized.   At present, money supply has not yet
increased to the same extent as in the early 60's.   And
with bumper harvests in agriculture, prices in farmers'
markets have not increased.   But, because prices for many
products deviate markedly from their values, coordination
prices begin to appear in the machine-building industry.
Coordination prices for many extra-plan products that are
produced in small local plants with high costs often
exceed plan prices.   For many scarce raw materials (such
as steel products and lumber) and agricultural sideline
products with low plan prices, negotiated buying and
selling prices are used to stimulate production and
satisfy people's livelihood needs.   If we are to use
market regulation, we should not interfere excessively
with coordination prices, negotiated buying and selling
prices, and other internal prices.   The best we can do is
to channel them in the right direction.   Our present plan
prices are actually far from stable.   If they are not
adjusted, it is possible that producing units may not try
to complete plan allocation assignments, but may sell
their products at negotiated prices.   Therefore, the
price level cannot remain stable if prices for many products consistently and substantially deviate from their
values.
        Last year, we raised the prices of certain agricul-
tural products in a planned way.   The price level increased by 5.8%.   As a result of chain reactions, the
actual increase might even be higher.   In addition, the
budget was out of balance and money supply increased a
little too fast.   These, to some extent, affected price
stability.   But price fluctuations this time are different from those in the three-year hardship period.   At
that time, prices in farmers' markets shot up substantially.   This time, prices are basically stable.   They
are even slightly lower than last year.   Therefore, it is
much easier to stabilize prices now than then.   We should
not be afraid of necessary and possible price adjustments
for the sake of price stability.   Of course, our present
price adjustment is by no means an easy task.   Because
the deviation of prices from values has been increasing
for more than ten years, it poses serious obstacles to
adjusting the proportional relations of the national
economy.   The extent of needed price adjustment is very
large.   Some price adjustments will adversely affect
people's livelihood or budgetary balance.   Therefore, we
must point out the clear direction of price adjustment
on the one hand, and proceed gradually starting from
those that pose the least disruption of people's livelihood and budgetary balance on the other.

1. What needs to be urgently adjusted and can be
    adjusted easily now are prices for producer
    goods, such as machine products and steel
    products. These are problems that urgently need
    to be resolved if circulation of producer goods
    is to be enlivened. In the past year or so,
    supply of machine products generally exceeded
    demand because of retrenchment in capital
    construction. Also, because prices were
    generally high and profits were generally large
    in this industry in the past, using the law of
    value as a regulator may result in more price
    decreases than price increases, so that price
    stability will not be affected. We should
    encourage enterprises (including companies) to
    negotiate coordination prices among themselves.
    These prices will facilitate adjustment of plan
    prices in the future. In the past two years,
    inventory of steel products increased markedly.
    It is necessary to reduce this inventory.
    Abundant products that have been overstocked for
    years should be sold at a discount. At the same
    time, prices for some scarce products should be
    appropriately increased. To do this, we should
    allow enterprises (we cannot disallow them,
    anyway) to negotiate buying and selling prices;
    and actively adjust our plan prices with
    reference to these prices so as to reduce
    overstocked inventory and encourage production
    of scarce products. At the same time, it is
    also necessary to change the method of setting
    prices for imported material resources so as to
    avoid conflicts with domestic prices. At pres-
    ent, prices for some imported commodities are
    fixed below domestic factory prices through sub-
    sidies by the Ministry of Foreign Trade. This
    is an extremely unreasonable practice. We
    should allow the Ministry of Foreign Trade to
    reduce or eliminate subsidies so as to reduce
    imports and protect domestic production.

The above-mentioned upward and downward price
adjustments need not adversely affect people's livelihood and price stability. Nor will they seriously
affect fiscal revenues. But, every item of price adjustment affects the distribution of profits between the
Center and localities, among localities, between industry
and commerce, between governments and enterprises, and
among enterprises. The resistance is very strong. We
must educate those in economic work to think from the
interests of the country, to submit partial interests
to overall interests, and to realize that this is an

irresistible trend in adjusting the national economy and
reforming the economic management system. Of course,
Central and local fiscal departments, as well as business
departments in charge, must consider the interests of all
regions, industries, and enterprises and adopt necessary
measures (such as changing the share of fiscal delivery
to higher authorities, share of retained profit, and
raising or lowering tax rates) to minimize losses to all
parties concerned. We should make everybody realize that
under the present price regime, the socialist economy
cannot grow up strong. Only by resolutely adjusting
prices, and reforming the whole economic management
system, can the socialist economy be freed from its present distorted pattern and develop in a healthy way.

2. Adjustment of prices for many producer goods
   affects the national economy and people's livelihood substantially and must be undertaken with
   care. Foremost is adjustment of prices for producer goods, such as coal and timber. These
   affect production costs of most enterprises,
   and ultimately people's livelihood. With our
   present shortage of energy sources, coal is
   China's most important source of energy. Prices
   for coal in China are about 50% lower than the
   world prices. The coal industry as a whole
   manages only to cover costs (including expenses
   related to maintaining simple reproduction) or
   turn a small profit. Close to half of the coal
   mines suffer losses. It is imperative that
   prices of coal be raised. But the steps to
   increase prices must be carefully arranged so as
   to avoid massive requests for price increase in
   other industries due to increase in cost. The
   negotiated prices for lumber are so much higher
   than plan prices that lumber producing areas are
   reluctant to deliver lumber to the state for
   unified allocation. They want to sell it on
   their own. If we forbid negotiated purchase and
   sales, we will have problems getting timber for
   furniture, building materials, and for packaging
   exported products. This problem must be carefully handled by phasing in price adjustment.
3. Purchase prices for agricultural products should
   continue to be raised as fiscal and economic
   conditions permit. At present, our purchase
   prices for agricultural products are still relatively low. Labor compensation for peasants
   is still markedly below that for workers. From
   the long view, we must still continue to raise
   purchase prices for food grain, and gradually
   reduce   and   finally   eliminate   reward   for

over-quota sales. After prices for food grain are raised, prices for other agricultural products must also be raised. Because last year's price increases were quite substantial, we do not have the means to raise prices again in the next two to three years. But, after prices were raised for food grain last year, prices among agricultural products have not yet been suitably adjusted. Therefore, in the next few years, it is still necessary to spend about 1 billion yuan to make reasonable adjustment in the prices for agricultural, forestry, livestock, fishery, and sideline products.

4. The most difficult adjustment relates to the selling prices for food grain, edible oil, cotton, and various subsidiary foodstuffs, because they greatly affect people's livelihood. Last year, when the buying prices for food grain, edible oil, and cotton were raised, their selling prices were not changed. The excess of buying prices over selling prices was subsidized by the government budget. Losses were also substantial in many subsidiary foodstuffs, including pork, eggs, and vegetables. According to an estimate by the General Price Bureau, these price subsidies for agricultural products reached 10 billion plus yuan, representing more than 10% of the government budget. The more agricultural products of these kinds are purchased, the greater will be the budget subsidies. As a result, the better the agricultural harvest, the more pressure is put on the budget. This phenomenon is abnormal. In some areas, the enthusiasm of commerce departments to buy these agricultural products has been affected. There are also serious conflicts arising from regional allocation which must depend on budget subsidies for their resolution. In the future, we must choose a suitable time to change these unreasonable conditions by raising the selling prices of food grain and edible oil, at least to the levels of their buying prices. At the same time, we must raise the selling prices of cotton and make suitable adjustment to the prices for cotton fabrics and blend fabrics. Losses on pork, eggs, and vegetables should be gradually reduced or even eliminated by improving operation methods. While raising prices for these products, the state must correspondingly raise wages by an amount equal to the current subsidies of 10 billion plus yuan. The difficulty of doing this is that

the effects of price increases vary according to
family size. If the state increases wages by an
amount equal to the price increases, about one-
third of the staff and workers will benefit,
one-third will suffer, and one-third will not be
affected one way or another. The one-third of
staff and workers who suffer are those with a
large number of dependents. The state must take
care of them. To reduce the percentage of suffering staff and workers to below ten, the state
must raise wages by more than the price
increases. But this will not only increase
budget expenditure, but also increase production
costs for industries. If it is not handled
well, it may even affect peace and solidarity.
Therefore, we should proceed with extreme
caution. But we cannot wait forever either. I
suggest that two to three years should be spent
in seriously studying this problem and coming up
with some feasible proposals. When production
has made enough headway, the proportional imbalance in the national economy has been largely
corrected, and budget and credit balance has
been achieved, we can then solve this long-
standing problem of prices.

In order to adjust prices without affecting price
stability, we should quickly formulate proposals for
early implementation with respect to price adjustment of
the first kind (machine products and steel products,
etc.). The way to do it is to allow regions, industries,
companies, and enterprises to set internal prices (such
as coordination prices and negotiated prices, etc.). In
fact, these adjustments have already been started at
lower levels. The only thing is that there have not been
corresponding changes in rules and regulations. What
they are doing is therefore justified but not legalized.
Without any rules for guidance, a certain amount of confusion is all but inevitable. Such confusion creates
opportunities for speculators and manipulators. We must
follow these informal changes with new rules and regulations. Or we can adopt some temporary measures to serve
as a frame of reference. As to price increases of the
second kind (coal and lumber, etc.), it is best that they
be gradually implemented in the next two to three years.
We should start searching for methods to adjust prices in
the second half of this year and phase them in in a
systematic way. As to price increases of the third and
fourth kinds (major livelihood means, such as food
grain), I am afraid they cannot be carried out before
adjustment of the national economy is basically completed. Since their effects on the budget and people's

livelihood are very great, and wages must be raised when
prices are increased, they can only be implemented when
production is better developed, and budget and credit
balance is achieved with some surplus. And since price
increases in this case are widely felt, repeated studies
should be undertaken within two to three years to come up
with feasible alternatives for the Center to choose.
(For example, should they be put into effect all at once,
or gradually?) Price departments should not drift along
in their old ways, nor should they take any hasty action.
Since these are important decisions relating to the
national economy and people's livelihood, all those involved in economic work and theoretical work in the
country should be mobilized to participate in discussion.

IV.   REFORM OF THE CURRENT PRICE CONTROL SYSTEM

China's economy is a socialist commodity economy
based on two kinds of socialist public ownership. Our
economic management system must combine plan regulation
with market regulation, and fully exploit the regulating
functions of the market under the guidance of the state
plan. In the past, our economic management system over-
emphasized plan control and ignored market regulation.
Correspondingly, our price control system also overem-
phasized the unified plan prices, and ignored the regulating functions of the law of value on prices. As a
result, adjustment of plan prices did not catch up with
changes in production conditions, with prices deviating
more and more from values. We have now begun to make
use of market regulation. Market regulation refers to
regulation by means of the law of value. When the law of
value is violated, market regulation cannot help us to
realize the state plan and ensure balance in market
supply and demand. On the contrary, it may even disrupt
the state plan and lead to proportional imbalance in the
national economy.

In the past year or more, we began to make use of
some market regulation and realized to our dismay that
deviation of prices from values conflicts everywhere with
adjustment of the national economy and reform of the
economic management system. Without changing the irrational conditions created by the current price system, we
are afraid to freely expand the scope of market regulation. Furthermore, we must adopt various administrative
measures (such as changing the share of retained profits
and providing financial subsidies) to counteract effects
resulting from the operation of the law of value. This
way, the economy will not be truly managed by economic
means (using objective economic laws). As adjustment of
the national economy is far from being completed at

present, some disturbances resulted from increases in the
buying prices for agricultural products and selling
prices for some products. To stabilize market prices, we
could not freely pursue adjustment of prices and reform
of the price control system. But like adjustment of
prices mentioned earlier, we cannot bide our time with
reform of the price control system. We should carry it
out in a planned and systematic manner.

From 1965 to 1966, we also raised the problem of
price adjustment. We formulated a five-year plan to
adjust prices. But at that time we were thinking of
adjusting through state plans under the sponsorship of
price departments. We did not think of relating it to
reform of the economic management system, especially
reform of the price control system. Experience in the
past 20 to 30 years shows that it is very difficult to
completely solve the problem of adjusting prices simply
through state plans. In the past 20 plus years, we
discussed the problem of prices almost every year except
in the several years when the "Cultural Revolution"
created the greatest turmoil. We also made some adjustments. But prices did not become more and more rational.
On the contrary, they deviated more and more from values.
The reason was that there were up to one million prices.
Cost calculation for each and every product was extremely
complicated. There were endless disputes between
producers and users with their divergent interests.
Therefore, no single price control agency, no matter how
competent, could hope to handle this complicated problem
well through subjective plans. Price adjustment this
time must fully utilize market regulation under the
guidance of state plans. This necessitates a thorough
reform of the current price control system to correspond
to reform of the whole economic management system.

The recent attempt to reform the economic management
system makes us deeply realize that current plan prices
have become obstacles to various reforms. We should not
limit ourselves to profit retention alone in our efforts
to expand enterprise autonomy. Rather, we should allow
enterprises to have the autonomy to adjust prices when
conditions are favorable. Enterprises should have the
power to raise prices for scarce products, reduce prices
for abundant products, and reduce prices to get rid of
overstocked material resources. Unified control should
be exercised over major livelihood means, such as food
grain, cotton fabrics, etc. But we can only set a standard price for textile products with their many varieties
and colors. We cannot hope to control the price of every
variety. The same applies to machine products and steel
products with their many varieties and specifications.
To overcome this problem, we can set up various specialized companies in the future and allow them to set prices

for different varieties, specifications, and colors under the guidance of price control departments. Coordination prices can be negotiated among companies. Buying and selling prices for many small commodities can be negotiated between producers and sellers. Price departments should comprehensively study price changes in the whole country, formulate an overall plan to adjust prices, and organize relevant departments to jointly regulate. They can also announce standard prices and magnitudes of fluctuations for important products according to market conditions to serve as references for relevant regions, departments, companies, and enterprises in their attempts to adjust prices. We should gradually transform price departments from agencies which set concrete prices to ones that determine the direction and policies of price adjustment, and supervise and guide prices.

We can consider increasing the power and responsibility of provincial governments over price control. There can be some price differentials among regions. Any disputes arising from this arrangement should be settled by the National General Price Bureau. Seasonal products can have season price differentials. The size of these differentials should reflect supply and demand conditions. Prices for new products can be set independently during the trial marketing period. These products can be sold independently or through commerce departments. To encourage replacement of old products by new products, prices for new products can be set higher (but subject to market demand) and prices for old products can be set lower. General commodities that are stocked in warehouses for more than one year should be sold at a discount. (Of course, there must be a certain reserve for scarce products.) In capitalist commodity exchanges, prices for some commodities vary from time to time in a given day. Prices for foodstuffs in supermarkets that are more than three days old are reduced automatically. Prices for many articles of daily use are reduced after three months. Even prices for consumer durables such as automobiles are reduced after some time. Our prices must be kept relatively stable. But they cannot remain unchanged either. Or great losses will result because overstocked material resources cannot be handled in time. In short, our prices must be both stable and flexible. After the system of unified revenues and unified expenditures and the system of unified purchase and guaranteed marketing are changed, and enterprises gain their necessary autonomy, they will see to it that prices will not be reduced at will. At the same time, with competition among enterprises, they will not raise prices at will, either.

Because we paid attention to plan regulation only and ignored market regulation for 20 plus years, many of

our enterprise managers do not understand the functions
of the law of value. Some confusion may result from the
adoption of market regulation. Therefore, fairly strict
control over prices must at present be exercised by price
departments and other economic management departments.
Existing confusion should be contained in time. At the
same time, all economic workers must be educated on how
to use the law of value. Just as comrade Mao Zedong
said, the law of value is a great school. It can teach
tens of millions of cadres to do a good job in economic
work. Leadership comrades in economic work must master
the art of using prices, tax rates, and interests as
economic levers to adjust the proportional relations of
the national economy. At present, we must combine price
adjustment with tax rate adjustment. For example, in the
case of coal and petroleum, because resource conditions
vary among mines and fields, price adjustment alone
without tax rate adjustment cannot eliminate the uneven
distribution of hardship and joy among mines and fields.
Comrades in price work have all the more reasons to
master the art of using the law of value to market-
regulate. For many years, our overreliance on plan
regulation and neglect of regulation through prices (law
of value) resulted in deviation of prices from values and
proportional imbalance in the national economy. In our
reform of the price control system, we should free ourselves from the bondage of natural economy[*3] thinking,
and honestly admit that our present economy is still a
socialist commodity economy and that we must be good at
maintaining the national economy in balance with market
regulation. A thorough reform of the price control
system should be gradually completed under the guidance
of this thought.

EDITOR'S NOTES

    *1. Unified revenues and unified expenditures
refers to a system of financial management in which all
profits and most depreciation charges of state enterprises are to be turned over to the state treasury. And
almost all capital expenditures, including quota circulating capital of state enterprises, are to be financed
interest free by the state treasury regardless of individual enterprise performance.
    *2. Unified purchase and guaranteed marketing is a
system of commodity circulation in which the state
attempts to monopolize the market outlets of producers
and the supply sources of users.
    *3. Natural economy is the opposite of commodity
economy. A natural economy produces for self-sufficiency
rather than for exchange.

8
Why Was the Budget in Deficit When the Production Situation Was So Good?

After reading the reports by comrades Yao Yilin and Wang Bingqian, many comrades feel that our national economy has turned "sunny" since the policy of "adjustment, reform, reorganization, and improvement" was announced in the Second Session of the Fifth National People's Congress. They think that our present economy looks very bright. But the big budget deficits seem like clouds that interrupt the otherwise clear sky. Where do these clouds come from? Will they bring rain? May they be causes for concern? Indeed, this is a new situation and new problem. I have thought this problem over again and again. Here I offer my views for your reference.

To clarify this problem, I think I must first talk about how the economic situation in last and this year should be evaluated and see if we can say that the situation looks bright.

My view is that the prospects are indeed bright. In this I have full confidence. But last and this year's situation cannot be said to be "bright." It can only be described as "turning from overcast to cloudy." We have been turned back from the "brink of disaster" from the ten-year catastrophe of the "Cultural Revolution," and have begun to correct the long-standing mistake of blindly pursuing quick success and high growth rate of output regardless of economic returns. But the losses and difficulties resulting from this ten-year catastrophe are as numerous as they are serious. These few years we are still just beginning to repay the old debts accumulated for 10 or 20 years. This debt cannot be repaid in two to three years. It can only be repaid in stages. At present, there are still many problems facing the state and the people's livelihood. We should honestly tell the people of the country both the promises and the

First published in People's Daily, September 2, 1980.

difficulties, and both the achievements and the inadequacies.

     But on the other hand, it is also true that our eco-
nomic situation is improving. How can we tell the
economic situation is improving? We must have some
scientific basis. For instance, the growth rate of our
industrial output was 14.3% in 1977 and 13.5% in 1978.
But it dropped to 8.5% once adjustment was started last
year. The planned growth rate for this and next year
will further decline to 6%. (This year's plan can be
overfulfilled.) Some comrades therefore think that the
situation is deteriorating. This view is not scientific.
It should be pointed out that the growth rates for 1977
and 1978 represented recovery. Also, they were not
solid. The long-standing mistake of blindly pursuing
high growth rate of output regardless of economic returns
had not been corrected in these two years. Because of
the blind pursuit of growth rate in industrial output,
capital construction was increasingly overextended. And
many construction projects had long gestation periods,
thus greatly reducing the economic returns of construction. Also, in order to complete output assignment,
nobody bothered with product quality and production
costs. Nobody even bothered to ask whether the products
meet the needs for national construction and people's
livelihood. In 1978, the amount of circulating capital
increased by 30 billion yuan. Most of it was spent on
overstocking material resources in warehouses. Production plans were overfulfilled and profits were turned
over to higher authorities. But the output could not be
used and added only to an overstocked inventory. Thus,
part of the profits turned over to higher authorities
were only account entries. They represented fiscal revenues financed with bank loans. Starting from 1979, an
inventory of overstocked material resources was made. As
a result, product quality and production costs improved
somewhat. Although the growth rate dropped slightly, it
was more solid. And economic returns of production
increased. Even so, last year's situation was still not
satisfactory. As we cleaned one batch from the old
overstock, we added another batch to the new overstock.
This year, we must change this resolutely. We must
resolutely stop production of goods that are not needed
by the market and users, even though the growth rate may
drop a little. This drop in the growth rate of output
can improve not only the economic returns of enterprise
production, but also the economic returns of construction
by facilitating retrenchment of capital construction.
The growth rate may seem to be dropping, but economic
returns are improving. As long as economic returns continue to improve, the growth rate will increase when
adjustment of the national economy is completed.

Now let us return to the question raised by all of us. That is, why are there such big budget deficits when adjustment begins to produce some results? This complicated problem needs to be analyzed from several aspects.

First, I think there are two major direct reasons for the big budget deficits. On the one hand, we need to greatly retrench investment in capital construction. But because of various difficulties, we have not succeeded in doing so. On the other hand, we must use a great deal of financial and material resources to repay the 20-year-old debt owed to people's livelihood. It is all but inevitable that the planned budget was exceeded, resulting in large deficits.

We can look back at the road we took in recent years. I think it is entirely correct that the Party Central Committee is resolutely carrying out the policy of "adjustment, reform, reorganization, and improvement" and taking adjustment as the key link. But it now appears that the results might have been even better if this policy had been announced one year earlier. In 1978, we still did not fully realize the long-standing mistake of blindly pursuing higher growth rate of output and expanding the scale of capital construction. It was not corrected in time. On the contrary, because the industrial and agricultural output situation was relatively strong, and fever went to our heads, we once again increased the budget provisions for capital construction by 50%, raising an already excessive accumulation rate to 36.5%. It approached the average figure of 39% for the three-year "Great Leap Forward" period. As a result, the long hidden proportional imbalance in our national economy was suddenly exposed. This time, the error was corrected relatively quickly. In the first half of 1979, it was decided that investment in capital construction in the state budget was to be reduced by 20%. But because many new construction projects were already started, most of the earmarked retrenchment could not be effected. This year, further retrenchment is planned in order to balance the budget. Investment for capital construction in the state budget has again been reduced by 30% from last year. Our determination is very strong. But many earmarked retrenchments have already been underway for more than a year. It is very difficult to recoup all the investment. In addition, because of the lack of strict control over investment by local governments and enterprises, their investment increased by more than what the Central government reduced. Therefore, the total investment in capital construction was slightly higher last year than the year before. This year, it may exceed that of last year. This is not only a very important reason for the appearance of budget deficits, but also detrimental to a basic adjustment of the proportional imbalance

in the national economy.   Therefore, this situation has
to be changed as soon as possible.   This requires that
the whole country from the top to the bottom make a
greater resolution to really reduce the total investment
in capital construction through joint efforts and
thoroughly turn this situation around in the next one to
two years.

On the other hand, the Center has resolved to
improve people's living standards, especially that of the
peasants, and has started to gradually repay a 20-year-
old debt.   This is entirely necessary.   And it produces
good economic and political impacts.   For peasants, in
addition to correcting the extreme Left line of the
"Gang of Four" and allowing plenty of autonomy to agricultural production teams, the purchase prices for agricultural products were increased by 22% last year.
Peasants' livelihood markedly improved in most regions.
For staff and workers, after 40% were promoted in 1977,
another 40% were promoted last year.   (Because of difficulties in evaluation, this promotion was postponed to
this year.   In some cases, it has not even started.)   A
large amount of bonuses were given out.   The Center estimated that these two items would increase fiscal expenditures by 10 billion yuan.   But the actual expenditures
exceed the planned figure by 4 billion plus yuan.   Also,
because last year's promotion of staff and workers did
not start until November and prices for some agricultural
products were not raised at all or enough and need to be
raised some more, these two items of expenditure are
expected to be higher this year than last year.   This is
an old debt that needs to be repaid.   We have repaid only
a small part so far.   We must continue to repay more as
fiscal conditions permit in the future.   Most people are
happy that the Center adopted these measures even under
difficult conditions.   But a small number of people, such
as people in poor rural villages who do not have surplus
food grain to sell or must depend on food grain resold
to them by the state, and low-wage staff and workers who
have not been promoted or received bonuses, still face
difficulties in their livelihood.   Under these conditions, we must be mindful of their hardship and take
care of them whenever conditions permit, on the one hand.
On the other hand, we must honestly explain to the people
the state's difficulties and mobilize them to tighten
their belts to help bring about an early smooth completion of the national economic adjustment.   Provided that
we sum up experience and lessons learned from the adjustment work, and thoroughly implement the adjustment policies decided upon by the Center since the Third Plenary
Session of the Party's Eleventh Central Committee, our
prospects are increasingly promising.

Second, these huge budget deficits are inseparable from our current economic management system, especially the financial and money management system. It can be said that these huge budget deficits expose the fundamental weaknesses of our institutions.

In order to clearly explain this point, a new question must first be raised. That is, in the past we often said finance was the concentrated expression of the economy. Why do unprecedentedly huge budget deficits appear when the economy begins to improve? The foremost reason is that under our present financial system, state finance often cannot directly reflect economic conditions. During the three-year "Great Leap Forward" period, many products with little or no use value were produced. The growth rate of output was high; fiscal revenues were large. But much of the output simply added to the inventory of useless products. In 1958, a year with the greatest waste, there was a budget surplus of 3.38 billion yuan. There was again a surplus of 2.54 billion yuan in 1959. A deficit of 1.92 billion yuan began to appear in 1960. At that time, the huge difficulties in the economy were manifested in financial terms because the accumulated inventory ate up a large amount of bank loans. In 1960, the money supply increased by 82% over that of 1957. In 1961, it was 1.4 times higher than in 1957. Because of price inflation, people withdrew their money from the banks to panic purchase. This time is different from the three-year hardship period. Last year, the budget deficit was as high as 17.06 billion yuan. But the increase in money supply was far less than this. The reason was that people's savings deposits not only did not decline, but increased by about 10 billion yuan. In addition, deposits by state enterprises increased by several billion yuan. Extra-budget deposits by local governments, and deposits of capital construction units, agencies, and armed forces, also increased. Because market supply (especially food supply) was more abundant than in past years, there was no queue buying apart from certain high-grade durables. Savings increased substantially. Many staff and workers and even peasants in affluent regions hoped to save enough money to buy television sets and other high-grade durables. In the first half of this year, these conditions continued. Money supply was slightly reduced. Comparing the end of June this year with the end of 1978, money supply increased only slightly faster than the volume of commodity circulation (including price hikes). It is estimated that money supply in the second half of this year will increase a little more.

Last year, because the purchase prices for agricultural products were raised, the state raised the selling prices of meat, eggs, and others correspondingly. Plan

prices were increased by 5.8% as a result. Because of
this, the state gave subsidies to staff and workers. In
1960 and 1961, because of excessive money supply and poor
harvests, prices at farmers' markets went up by leaps and
bounds. In the recent two years, not only did prices at
farmers' markets not go up, they came down slightly
instead. In some regions, farmers' market prices for
pork and eggs were lower than plan prices. This summer,
the state was forced to lower prices for pork and eggs to
sell them. But, at the same time, we can see that
because the purchasing power of urban and rural residents
has increased significantly, supply of some commodities
is still quite short. In addition, the pursuit of ille-
gal profits by enterprises with their expanded autonomy
has led to serious open and disguised price hikes.
People are unhappy about that. And the state is adopting
measures to stop it. At present, control of prices for
vegetables is the least satisfactory. The peasants think
that purchase prices are too low. The staff and workers
think that selling prices are too high. The state
meanwhile keeps losing money. I think we should study
carefully the management system to come up with a solution to eliminate the huge waste in the buying and
selling process.

     Our present price system is very irrational. It is
one of the reasons for the huge budget deficits during
adjustment. To avoid market confusion, prices have been
frozen for 12 years, since the beginning of the "Cultural
Revolution." As a result, prices for various products
greatly deviate from their values. This leads to great
difficulty in our present efforts to use market regulation. Irrational prices also lead to budget imbalance.
At present, buying prices exceed selling prices for food
grain and a number of agricultural products. Budget subsidies for these items alone exceed 20 billion yuan a
year. To stabilize prices and secure people's livelihood, the state still cannot raise the selling prices of
these products. As a result, the more food grain and
edible oil are purchased in some regions, the greater the
amount of budget subsidies required. Twenty years ago,
as long as agricultural harvests were good, fiscal revenues markedly increased. The present conditions are different. On the one hand, bumper harvests increase the
availability of light industrial raw materials. With
higher light industrial output, fiscal revenues increase.
On the other hand, bumper harvests also increase budget
subsidies and reduce revenues. These conditions cannot
continue for too long. After the state has balanced the
budget with some real surplus, it is necessary to raise
the selling prices of these products while raising wages
correspondingly. At present, the state still cannot
afford to raise wages substantially. It must resign

itself to continuing these subsidies and refrain from
raising the prices of these products. But if this
problem is not resolved, it will create problems for the
budget balance. It think it is necessary to explain this
problem to the people clearly.

Finally, I will talk about our present economic
management system, especially the financial and money
management system. The system of "eating from the free
communal kitchen" and government responsibility has been
too well entrenched to be changed. Now the system of
unified revenues is beginning to break down. But the
system of unified expenditures is still intact. This is
also one reason why budget deficits cannot be eliminated
for the time being. At present, most of the investment
in capital construction is financed by budget appropriations. Even quota circulating capital is financed by
budget appropriations. If these two items of capital
funds are financed by bank loans, budget deficits will be
greatly reduced. In the past, bank loans could not be
used for capital construction or quota circulating capital. Because both investment funds for capital construction and quota circulating capital are provided free of
charge, enterprises are not motivated to economize on
capital construction investment and reduce inventory of
commodities. As a result, huge waste is inevitable.
Annual losses from these sources amount to several
billion yuan. The state has decided to convert investment in fixed assets into bank loans and charge interest
on them and quota circulating capital on a trial basis
starting next year. Banks will be allowed to make a
small amount of loans for capital construction, especially for enterprises to tap potentials, renovate, and
retrofit. This year, several billion yuan have been
appropriated to serve as circulating capital for newly
constructed enterprises and as funds for old enterprises
to tap potentials, renovate, and retrofit. In the
future, we can consider shifting this financing to banks.
This way, fiscal expenditures can be greatly reduced.
Also, economic returns from capital construction investment and enterprise production operation can be raised,
leading to higher state budget revenues.

Treasury departments of capitalist countries are not
responsible for investment. Internal funds often represent less than half of the capital investment in enterprises. The rest of the investment is financed by bank
loans. Enterprise circulating capital is entirely
financed by bank loans. Since enterprises must constantly pay back loans and interests, they must ensure
rapid turnover of these funds without any waste. At
present, Yugoslavia is adopting similar systems. China
inherited the financial management method used by the
Soviet Union in the 50's which led to a very slow turn-

over of funds. Other people make use of one dollar as if
it were two dollars. We use two dollars as if they were
one dollar. More seriously, under this free supply
system, a large amount of useless machines, equipment,
and unwanted products inevitably accumulates and
deteriorates in warehouses. If we don't make up our
minds to change this inefficient and wasteful method of
allocating funds, we may still have budget deficits two
to three years from now. That is why the Center is
seriously studying ways to reform the economic management
system, especially the financial and money management
system, hoping to make significant reforms within two to
three years that will eliminate budget deficits.

Here, it is necessary to emphasize the significance
of exercising the lever effect of socialist banks. We
all know that capitalist state banks play an important
role in economic development. Banks not only collect
scattered and unused funds from the people for investment, they also regulate the amount and direction of
investment by changing interest rates and credit availability. The state exercises some plan regulation
through banks. Because our banks are not allowed to make
loans for capital construction, and interests are not
charged on quota circulating capital, they become essentially cashiers and treasury agents of finance departments. They do not exercise any economic regulation at
all. Under a system which is concerned only with plan
regulation and not with market regulation, this banking
system is accepted by the people without any question.
It may even be regarded as a sign of socialist
superiority or an embodiment of some "objective law."
After market regulation is extensively employed, banks,
like prices, must become an important regulating lever.
Through bank regulation, not only can the turnover rate
of funds be greatly increased, waste can also be reduced,
thus greatly improving economic returns from production
and construction. Of course, this requires not only a
fundamental change in our economic management system, but
also an improvement in the economic knowledge and operation and management know-how of tens of millions of
economic management personnel. Therefore, this reform
will take some time. It is not possible to complete this
reform in two to three years. Economic reform requires
not only clear direction and strong determination, but
also steady advance along a thorny new trail.

In summary, our country had just recovered from a
severe and lingering illness that has afflicted us for
many years. The Center has found the cures for this illness. But complete recovery will take some time. At
present, there are two major tasks ahead of us. There
are also two major problems. One is adjustment. Another
is reform. Adjustment is only half completed. It will

take several more years to clear up the sequelae. Reform has just been started. Although some initial results have been achieved, such a fundamental reform of the economic structure requires us to rack our brains to break a new path of our own. We can, of course, learn from other countries. But there is no one ready-made economic model that suits our conditions completely and that we can adopt without any modification. Also, we can no longer adopt the early 50's method of wholesale borrowing from other people. The Center's correct policies must still be constantly perfected through summing up experience during practice. It is still not an easy task to make the people of the whole country, especially the leadership cadres in economic work, familiar with the Center's policies and resolutely implement them wholeheartedly. But we can be certain of one thing. That is, our economic situation is improving and our prospects are bright.

9
An Inquiry into Reform of the Economic System

In the past, the greatest weakness of our national economic management system was to replace economic management with administrative management. There was only plan regulation, and no market regulation. After the Third Plenary Session of the Party's Eleventh Central Committee, it was proposed that plan regulation be combined with market regulation. What actually is plan regulation? What is market regulation? How can these two be combined? There are diverse views on these. Here I will only talk about my views.

Market regulation developed with the emergence of commodity economy. In feudal societies, the economy was basically self-sufficient. Although market existed, its functions were minimal. In capitalist societies, market regulation assumed a major role. Market regulation actually is the maintenance of balance between market demand and supply by relying on the regulating functions of the law of value. The socialist society develops from the capitalist society. Therefore, many things in the capitalist society must be inherited and reformed. They cannot be totally negated. Its producive forces (including science and technology) must in the main be inherited. Its production relations must be reformed (such as the establishment of public ownership over means of production and the adoption of planned management of the national economy), but many things (including most of enterprise management and part of market regulation) must also be inherited. Capitalist countries have 200 to 300 years of proven experience in enterprise management. This experience should be inherited in large part. Of course, we cannot inherit the exploitive relations between the bourgeoisie and the proletariat. But we must

First published in Economic Research, 1980, No. 6.

still learn from their experience in organizing and managing plants. We must also partly inherit market regulation because, like capitalist societies, we are engaged in large-scale social production. Ours is not a self-sufficient natural economy. It is a commodity economy. In large-scale social production of commodities, relations among industries and enterprises are extremely complex. It is not possible to do away with market regulation. Of course, capitalist market regulation aims at promoting free competition. Our market regulation operates under planned guidance. We must realize that as long as commodity production and commodity exchange exist, market regulation cannot be done away with. Marx thought that in a mature socialist economy, commodity and money relations could be done away with. Practice has proved that it is still not possible to do so. When the Soviet Union was first founded, war-time communism was practiced. There was an attempt to do away with commodity and money relations. Later, it was found out that in countries where the peasant economy still dominated, commodity and money relations must be used and not be done away with. Therefore, Lenin adopted the New Economic Policy later on. This policy was designed to fully utilize commodity and money relations. In China, where capitalism has not been fully developed, commodity economy cannot be done away with after the socialist system has been established; it must still be developed in a big way. Among the total population of the country, peasants represented 90% in the beginning of the republic. They still represent some 80% at present. Of the food grain produced, more than three-fourths are used for their own consumption (food, seeds, animal feed, etc.). The state purchases only about 20%. Therefore, in most of China, the semi-self-sufficient peasant economy still predominates. Social production is still at a very low level. These conditions also make many comrades wonder how market regulation can be implemented. But Shanghai and certain large cities have rich experience in market regulation because of their well-developed capitalism in the past.

How market regulation can be fully utilized under the control of state plans sounds like a new problem and many comrades feel we do not have the experience. In fact, China has rich experience in this respect, at least much richer than when the Soviet Union was first founded. When New China was founded, many economic components co-existed. In the winter of 1949, the capitalist economy still dominated the market. Most commodities in the market were still supplied by capitalist industry and commerce. At that time, we were engaged in a struggle with capitalist industry and commerce. The first struggle was to stabilize prices. We did not resort to

administrative means (coercion).   Instead, we adopted
economic means by relying on objective economic laws.
This struggle was waged mainly in Shanghai.   It was a
fierce struggle.   Our victory was complete.   Following
this, we adopted order-placing, unified purchase, and
guaranteed marketing, and expanded joint public and
private operation to whole trades.   Administrative orders
were not used in this struggle either.   Instead, the law
of value and the law of surplus value were used to wage a
fierce struggle against capitalist industry and commerce
in the market.   We won one victory after another and
forced them to accept socialist transformation.   Through
placing orders with them and acting as their agents, we
forced capitalist industry and commerce to produce and
operate according to the state plan.   Through supply and
marketing cooperatives, we controlled rural markets.
We used price policy to make individual peasants produce
according to the state plan.   Thus, a solid foundation
was laid for planned management of the national economy
after 1953.
     In the First Five-Year Plan period, plan regulation
of the national economy played an increasingly important
role.   But before the three great transformations were
completed and when joint public and private operation was
first established over whole trades (at that time there
were large numbers of financially independent so-called
"public and private jointly operated" shops and handicraft cooperatives), market regulation still played a
very important role.   Some comrades said that because
centralized management was adopted in the First Five-Year
Plan, things went very well and developed very fast.   In
fact, it was due to a combination of plan regulation with
market regulation, with plan regulation assuming a dominant role.   In 1956 and 1957, although cooperativization
was started, the degree of cooperativization was still
very low.   In short, what was practiced was not entirely
plan regulation.   It was a very flexible application of
it.   Starting from 1958, under the premise that the
faster and more thorough socialist transformation was,
the better it became, people's communes were widely set
up in rural areas.   In urban areas, financially independent shops under "joint public and private operation" and
handicraft cooperatives were eliminated.   For example, in
the past the Dongan Market was composed of many small
shops, each with their own unique features.   Later it was
changed into the Dongfeng Market.   All its unique
features disappeared as a result.   It merely became a
second department store.   Handicraft cooperatives were
transformed into cooperative plants.   They were no longer
financially independent and bonuses were no longer
distributed according to labor.   Instead, fixed wages
were adopted and profit was sent to the government.

Therefore, big collective enterprises actually were transformed into small whole people enterprises. Thus, socialist public ownership dominated the whole country. At the same time, because we adopted the Soviet Union's method of planned management, enterprise, commune, and brigade autonomy was reduced to the minimum. Since revenues and expenditures were unified in fiscal matters, and unified purchase and guaranteed marketing were adopted in commerce, only plan regulation was emphasized from then on. The role of market regulation was increasingly reduced, resulting in increasing rigidity in economic management. At present, most comrades realize that it is imperative that the existing economic management system be changed and that market regulation be fully utilized under the control of the state plan. But, some comrades still think that there are conflicts between plan regulation and market regulation. Where plan regulation is practiced, market regulation cannot co-exist. And where market regulation is practiced, plan regulation cannot exist. Therefore, they frequently ask how the scopes of plan regulation and market regulation can be defined. I think this perception is wrong. Plan regulation and market regulation can co-exist and supplement each other. They are not irreconcilable opposites. The reason why such a doubt arises is because we have a wrong conception about plan regulation. We think that the only correct model of socialist planned management is that system of planned management copied from the Soviet Union in the early 50's which was characterized by strict and rigid controls.

In the past, many comrades studied the Soviet Union's system of planned management as practiced in the early 50's. They thought that planned management must consist of only unified revenues and expenditures and unified purchase and guaranteed marketing. In fiscal matters, the Ministry of Finance should centralize control. In commerce, the Ministry of Commerce should monopolize operation. Industry must produce and market according to plan. Industrial enterprises were completely cut off from the market and users. All economic activities were controlled by several Central ministries. Localities, enterprises, and communes all acted according to plan. They did not need to think for themselves at all. When I investigated in Jiangsu, many comrades at the provincial level said that the provincial plan was nothing more than a sum of all the plans sent to them by the Central ministries. The province could not make adjustment and hence did not need to use its brains. Comrades in the cities of Wuxi and Changzhou commented that the sum of the plans sent to them by the provincial bureaus amounted to their cities' plans. There was no room for adjustment and no need to rack their brains.

The only thing to do was to carry out the plan. Was this really planned management? Should socialist planned management be practiced in this manner? I think there is room for doubt. In theory, socialism means that people of the whole country are masters. That means they have to use their brains. But in fact, apart from several Central organs in charge, nobody else could be masters and make decisions. In particular, enterprises, communes, and brigades had no autonomy. They could only carry out what the state plan told them to do. As to the management power of the laboring people, there was nothing to speak of. Was this really in line with Marx's socialist principle? Is it better to have "a lot of brains up there and no brains down here," or to let enterprises, communes, and brigades use their brains and let the laboring people make suggestions? The latter approach is undoubtedly better. The question is, if the autonomy of enterprises, communes, and brigades is accepted, how can the status of planned management be guaranteed? The way to do this is: "big plan, small freedom"; "centralize major power, decentralize minor power." The Center should control comprehensive balance of the national economy, and maintain a proper proportional relation between accumulation and consumption. That is to say, it should determine the size of capital construction, control major construction projects, take care of people's livelihood, and adjust the proportional relations between agriculture and light and heavy industries, and the proportional relations within industry and agriculture. If the budget is in balance, loan extensions and loan repayments are in balance, supply of and demand for material resources are in balance, and the foreign exchange market is in balance, then the rest could well be left alone to take their own courses with no fear of any major trouble. At present, our trouble is mainly due to the fact that there is no comprehensive balance. The state plan should be concerned with comprehensive balance. But we have not done a good job in this respect. Instead, it has concerned itself with individual concrete items and overlooked the proportional relation between accumulation and consumption. The result is that on the one hand everybody wants to hurry up and do it big by increasingly enlarging the size of capital construction; on the other hand, heavy industry develops too fast at the expense of agriculture and light industry. Thus, there is a shortage of both producer goods and consumer goods. Confusion is inescapable.

After the Third Plenary Session of the Party's Eleventh Central Committee, the Center recognized this problem and proposed to adjust the proportional relation between accumulation and consumption, reduce the size of capital construction, and raise people's living standards. Last year, purchase prices for agricultural and sideline products were raised substantially, thus increasing peasants' incomes. Also, 40% of staff and workers were promoted in 1977. Last year, another 40% of staff and workers were promoted. Bonuses were also paid out. All these raised the relative share of consumption and reduced the share of capital investment. It should be pointed out that the policy of reducing capital investment, raising people's living standards, particularly that of peasants, increasing peasants' incomes, and adjusting the proportional relation between accumulation and consumption is entirely correct. Some problems arose, mainly because comprehensive balance was not properly implemented. It is not possible to avoid all problems.

Some comrades question whether the adjustments have been correct or whether they have been properly carried out. They have doubt about the current situation. I think last year's situation was better than that of the previous year. First, the rural situation was greatly improved. Peasants' income actually increased. In the past, pork was quantitatively rationed. At present, pork is freely available. In Zhejiang province, it used to be very difficult to purchase live hogs. There were purchase quotas. Now there is no need for them. There is a long line of peasants waiting to sell live hogs to the state. The 1978 rural situation was better than that of 1977. And 1979 was better than 1978. With peasants representing 80% of the total population in the country, an improvement in their incomes and living standards is a major indication that the situation is good. Second, urban staff and workers received higher incomes and bonuses. Although prices for pork, eggs, and a few other things did increase, the state issued price subsidies. Also, there were a lot more goods in the market. Pork was readily available for unrestricted purchase. Supply of other goods was also more abundant. Compared with the three-year period of natural calamities, the situation is vastly different. A more abundant supply of agricultural and sideline products in the urban areas indicates that the situation is good. In addition, bank deposits increased substantially. This was rare in past years. Deposits by localities and enterprises increased. Communes and brigades used to borrow money every year. But last year, deposits exceeded loans. Savings by urban and rural residents also increased substantially. Last year, national income increased markedly. But income distribution underwent changes. Which of these changes are good and which are bad deserve further study. Therefore, it is wrong to think that the work has been poorly done and the situation is bad. The actual conditions just do not substantiate this assessment.

Our history has been full of disputes on tightening and relaxing controls. It seems that it is very difficult to strike a balance between these two extremes. According to my understanding, we never relaxed our control over the autonomy of enterprises, communes, and brigades in the 20 years between 1958 [sic] and 1976. The relaxation for several years after 1958 did expand local power to some extent. The confusion during this period was not due to excessive local power. Rather, it was because the Center wanted to do it big and fast without first taking care of comprehensive balance. It blindly sped up the growth rate of heavy industry by expanding the size of capital construction. In those few years, the proportion of accumulation was increased to about 40%. In those years, output from heavy industry increased by 2.5 times. And agricultural output decreased. Under the guidance of this mentality, local areas all jumped on the bandwagon. This serious imbalance in the national economy was bound to lead to confusion even if power had not been decentralized. The serious confusion in the national economy before 1976 did not result from relaxation of control, but mainly from sabotage by the "Gang of Four." Because this proportional imbalance has not yet been corrected even now, some confusions still persist. In order to adjust and reorganize, control must still be centralized in some respects. Thus, we cannot give free reins to reforming the economic management system. In order to adjust and reorganize, we can only take smaller and steadier steps in our institutional reform at present. We must test it in pilot projects before we extend our experience. We should never waiver in our confidence and determination in reform. Big confusion should be avoided as much as possible. But small confusion is all but unavoidable. Small confusion may even be beneficial because it exposes contradictions. Once contradictions are exposed, we are forced to use our brains to come up with solutions. In the past, both revenues and expenditures were guaranteed in fiscal matters, and both purchase and marketing were unified in industry. On the surface, there did not seem to be any contradictions. But, in fact, there was too much rigidity. If we want reform, we must be prepared for confusion. But there should not be big confusion. At present, some centralized and unified measures are temporary in nature. They are intended to correct and punish deviations. But they should not be regarded as permanent in nature.

Take for example the present confusions in prices and wages. Many comrades think that if control over prices is relaxed, there will be many uncontrollable price increases. In fact, price increases result from fiscal imbalance, excessive money supply, and excessive social purchasing power. At present, our power over price control has not been decentralized. Thus, price increases are not related to decentralization of power. Control over farmers' markets is a bit lax at present. But market prices have not increased to the same extent as in 1960 and 1961. On the contrary, they have decreased slightly. In some places, prices for pork, beef, and lamb meat are lower than state posted prices. In 1960 and 1961, prices increased due to excessive money supply. When we reduced capital investment, and retired several billion <u>yuan</u> of money through selling high-priced goods, market prices came down one after another. Prices for high-priced goods also fell until they were sold at par. In capitalist countries, industry and commerce set their own prices. If money supply is not excessive, prices are fairly steady. If our money supply is not excessive, our general price level can be kept stable even though individual prices may rise and fall. At present, there is quite a bit of confusion over bonuses. This is related to confusion in enterprise management and the fact that many staff and workers have not received any wage increases for more than ten years. Price adjustments and wage system reform since the Third Plenary Session of the Party's Eleventh Central Committee have had far more positive effects than negative effects on production development. In the future, prices must be further adjusted and the wage system must be further reformed. The principle of exchange of equal values and distribution according to labor must be more properly followed. We will not be able to stimulate peasants' and workers' production activism and produce at high speed if we insist on strictly maintaining the status quo.

Of course, ours is a socialist country. We cannot adopt a policy of laissez faire like a capitalist country. We must adopt planned management of the national economy. The central task of planned management is to bring about comprehensive balance in the national economy. In the past 20 years, there were several mistakes in our economic work. Apart from sabotage and interferences from Lin Biao and the "Gang of Four," the major reason was that we did not do a good job in comprehensively balancing the national economy, thus leading to proportional imbalance in the national economy. After New China was established, our national economy was in balance in the first eight years. Industrial and agricultural output grew very fast. People's living standards were gradually improved. We did not have any doubt about the superiority of socialism. In the following 20 years, apart from interferences and sabotage from Lin Biao and the "Gang of Four," we made two mistakes. One was that we made wrong plans for some years, leading to proportional imbalance in the national economy.

Another was that planned management was too rigidly applied, thus preventing the superiority of socialism from being developed. Now that management power is to be gradually decentralized, the Center must still control comprehensive balance. The state determines the total size of investment. Major construction projects must be decided on or approved by the Center to be included into a unified plan. Localities and enterprises should be permitted to decide on local medium and small projects, particularly projects to tap potentials, renovate, and retrofit in old enterprises. But these investments should also be included into the total accumulation fund. The state should announce control figures for localities to follow. If there is no limitation, localities and enterprises will all want to do it big and fast. The result may be to overshoot the state plan, leading to proportional imbalance in the national economy. Total labor employment and wages should also be determined by the state. Localities and enterprises are then free to make concrete arrangements according to announced control figures. Our experience in past years showed that the state must properly handle the relation between national construction and people's livelihood so that the sum of accumulation fund and consumption fund does not exceed total national income. This is the most important problem to be solved by plan regulation.

The key to market regulation is to expand the number of circulation channels, and to break down the monopoly enjoyed by material resources departments over producer goods, by commerce departments over urban consumer goods, by supply and marketing cooperatives over agricultural and sideline products, and by the Ministry of Foreign Trade over foreign trade. As production develops and as supply and demand become more balanced, we should gradually reduce the scope of plan allocation of producer goods and of unified purchase and guaranteed marketing of consumer goods. Among producer goods, with the exception of material resources in bulk quantities (such as whole sets of equipment, coal, petroleum, etc.) which are to be directly supplied according to the state plan through contracts between producers and users, material resources in general can be supplied by establishng an extensive network according to specialties as determined by material resources departments. Some ministries, bureaus, and big companies can also set up their own sales organizations. Center cities can also host trade fairs and adopt many different forms to facilitate exchange. With the exception of food grain, fabrics, and edible oil, quantitative rationing of other consumer goods should be phased out. Unified purchase and guaranteed marketing should be changed into contract orders and selective purchasing for commodities in

general. Plants should be allowed to sell on their own
the commodities that commerce departments do not
purchase. Supply and marketing cooperatives, communes,
and brigades should be allowed to sell their products in
urban areas. In short, the number of circulation channels should be increased and the number of circulation
links should be reduced so that contacts between producers and users can be facilitated. Will these measures
disrupt the unified socialist market? No. China's state
commerce has a solid material foundation. Even before
the socialist transformation of private industry and commerce was completed, it already exercised a firm control
over the national market. To allow some state plants,
communes, and brigades to sell their own products now can
only supplement state commerce, and will in no way under-
mine its leadership position, or disrupt the unified
socialist market. Some market competition is good for
breaking down bureaucratism in commerce and helping the
people. It is also conducive to improving product
quality, increasing product variety, increasing peasants'
income, and improving urban supply. Our urban and rural
residents will welcome it.
     In addition to increasing the number of circulation
channels, market regulation should also fully use the
functions of prices, tax rates, and credit. The state
should change prices and tax rates to encourage enterprises (including plants, communes, and brigades) to
increase production of certain scarce products, or to
reduce production of certain abundant products so as to
achieve balance between supply and demand. In addition,
bank credit should be judiciously used to direct
enterprise development through loans and interest rates.
Capitalist countries rely mainly on banks to regulate the
national economy. They encourage or restrict enterprise
investment through changes in money supply and interest
rates. They can also assist or discourage certain
industries through credit policy. Investment in
socialist countries is mainly handled through state
planning. But small investment can also be handled
through bank loans. A change from budget appropriations
to bank loans for capital construction can encourage
construction units to economize on capital funds.
Imposing full interest payments on circulating capital
can force enterprises to reduce inventory overstocking.
To facilitate commodity circulation, we should consider
reintroducing several kinds of commercial credit
arrangements, such as advance deposits, bank bills of
exchange, discount on promissory notes, private remit-
tances, and interest-bearing deposits by agencies and
enterprises. These arrangements will facilitate circulation of capital funds and guarantee commercial credit.
Banks will then no longer be cashier agencies for the

Ministry of Finance and will be better able to serve socialist economic development.

II. HOW TO ENLIVEN THE NATIONAL ECONOMY

Because our control was too restrictive in the past, it is therefore now necessary to enliven the national economy through institutional reform. In general, there are three alternatives. One alternative is to basically maintain the status quo. The Center still centralizes control. Some power is decentralized to localities. Enterprise autonomy in particular is to be expanded. Thus, it is still a minor change. A second alternative is to decentralize most power to localities. Localities are in control while enterprise power is appropriately expanded. The third alternative is to adopt mainly economic measures by managing the economy with economic organizations. A sizable portion of power is decentralized to enterprises under the guidance of state planning. Of course, the Center should still control what it should control, and localities should control what they should control. But the emphasis is on expanding the management power of enterprises. There have been disputes over these alternatives. Most comrades now accept the third alternative. I did some investigation in Jiangsu last year. Jiangsu is a pilot province for local responsibility. I wanted to study the advantages and disadvantages of local responsibility by enlarging provincial power. Jiangsu's experiment with enlarging local management power by adopting fiscal responsibility can be said to be successful. But I got different reactions from people in Wuxi, Changzhou, and Suzhou. They said since the Center adopted the policy of local responsibility for Jiangsu province, the province should also adopt the same policy towards them. They wanted to expand the power of their municipalities and counties. Later, I talked to people in eight enterprises to see what they thought. They said it did not matter whether the Center or localities were in control. All they knew was that enterprises were not allowed to exercise their own control. The key should be enterprise management power. After repeated consideration since my return, I feel that this position is quite reasonable. If enterprises do not have autonomy but are like beads on an abacus which can only move passively to wherever directed, then control will be too restrictive. It does not matter whether the Center or localities are in control.

In fact, people also have different views on the third alternative. The Central ministries feel that it is not a matter of all powers being centralized. Rather

some powers are overcentralized and others are under-
centralized. What should be centralized must still be
centralized. What should be decentralized must definitely be decentralized. Take for example the case of
planning departments. This year investment is to be
reduced. If we decentralize power to provinces, they may
want to increase investment. If power is further decentralized to enterprises, they may increase investment
by an even greater amount. Doesn't everybody want to tap
potentials, renovate, and retrofit?   Therefore, it is
imperative that capital investment planning be centralized. Some people complain that control over material
resources is too centralized and too strict. But material
resources departments say that they only control 10% to
20% of all material resources. Most of them are stocked
up in the warehouses of various ministries, bureaus, and
enterprises. If you want material resources to be efficiently allocated, most of the material resources should
be concentrated in the hands of material resource departments, much like commerce departments' control over
consumer goods. Therefore, control must still be centralized. All these views are valid. And they represent
the views of Central ministries. Therefore, their "third
alternative" is "a third alternative" that is somewhat
close to the first alternative.
     Localities favor expansion of local autonomy. They
want not only two-level fiscal management, but also
three-level fiscal management as far as municipalities
and counties are concerned. Fiscal management by level
will lead to many new problems. And enterprises will in
turn want to have separate fiscal management power. If
the Center does not control large enterprises such as
Anshan Steel and Daqing Oilfields and centralize their
profit, but instead decentralizes control over them to
localities, it is very difficult to guarantee fiscal
revenues to the Center. But if Anshan Steel is to be
controlled at the Center by the Ministry of Metallurgy,
should the several hundred plants in Liaoning province
that serve Anshan Steel be controlled by the Ministry of
Metallurgy also? Definitely not. If they are not controlled by the Ministry of Metallurgy, but are still controlled by localities, then some plants may not want to
guarantee their coordination tasks with Anshan Steel.
They may instead make their own arrangements for maximum
local benefits. Then how can Anshan Steel's coordination
tasks be guaranteed? Should the Ministry of Metallurgy
then coordinate hundreds of plants? That is also out of
the question.
     There are also problems related to local control.
China has 29 provinces and municipalities (excluding
Taiwan province). If they are divided into 29 regions
and 29 plans, then it is hard to ensure that economic

relations among regions will not be severed. Nor is it easy to prevent parochialism. The emergence of parochialism will definitely strangle the economy. If even nine countries in Europe are forming a common market, then it does not make sense for us as a country not to form a "common market," but to form isolated markets. This violates laws of economic development, particularly laws of modern economic development. For example, Shanghai is an economic center of the southeast and the whole country. If the linkages between Shanghai and the rest of the country are severed, then Shanghai cannot survive. This is not only bad for Shanghai, but also bad for the rest of the country. Therefore, the second alternative is also out of the question.

Fiscal management by level requires that industry also be managed by level, because industrial profit is the major source of fiscal revenues. If two-level or three-level management is adopted in industry, then it may present obstacles to forming specialized companies for coordinated specialization. For example, if a nationwide (or trans-provincial) automobile company is to be formed, then it would be necessary to pool all the efforts of up to 1,000 plants under the respective juris-dictions of Central ministries, provinces, municipali-ties, and counties. If the Party and government organs at various levels would not relinquish their control for fear of losing their share of the profit, then it would be extremely difficult to change from administrative management to economic management with respect to indus-try. Thus, the chance of ever realizing the general direction of reforming economic institutions is in doubt. Also, at present, part of enterprise profit goes to the Center and part of it goes to localities. This arrange-ment leads to many unresolvable conflicts between industry and commerce, and between industry and foreign trade. In the future, we must consider replacing this system of profit delivery with income tax collection. So much of income tax goes to the Center, and so much goes to localities. Whether this will in turn lead to new problems is difficult to say. In short, we have still not completely clarified our direction of reform. Many questions require further studies.

Because reform involves the interests of various regions, departments, and enterprises, there are frequent disagreements among Central ministries, between Central ministries and provinces, municipalities, and autonomous regions, between rich and poor provinces, between provin-ces and the districts, municipalities, and counties under their jurisdiction, between all the above and enter-prises, and between rich and poor enterprises. We can only take care of the overall situation and handle these

conflicts under the premise of accelerating the realiza-
tion of the four modernizations. My view is that at
present no single method of institutional reform can be
adopted for the country as a whole, as conditions vary
from region to region. How should we go about institutional reform? For example, Sichuan has done a good job
in institutional reform. Relative to the whole country,
Sichuan is a region with a medium level of development.
It is representative of the whole country. Its social
production has not reached a high level. It has not
developed any specialized companies, joint corporations,
trusts, and syndicates. Therefore, its major concern is
with the question of enterprise autonomy. Its reform
starts with enterprises as the basic unit and gradually
proceeds to joint ventures mainly within the province.
Shanghai is an advanced region. In old China, Shanghai
had the highest level of capitalist development. At
present, its level of social production is quite high.
Also, Shanghai has linkages with the rest of the country.
Therefore, the method of institutional reform in Shanghai
is different from that used in Sichuan. It has already
developed trusts and syndicates. Institutional reform
based entirely on enterprises is no longer suitable.
Companies and enterprises should be jointly reformed
within the scope of industries and companies. Shanghai
has the advantage of an early start in matters of institutional reform. In fact, some reforms in Shanghai (such
as trade fairs for producer goods, free markets for agricultural and sideline products) have already spread to
other provinces and municipalities. In general, these
are very useful to enlivening circulation channels for
producer goods and consumer goods. But because they have
attracted other people's scarce material resources or
even products targeted for planned purchase, some
conflicts are unavoidable. These conflicts should be
resolved through negotiation and not retaliation. Last
year, Shanghai used its own capital funds, machines,
equipment, and technical resources to establish joint
enterprises (compensation trade) with other provinces
bringing benefits to both parties. I think this activity
should be encouraged. Many countries in Western Europe
are organizing common markets. Our provinces should
strengthen cooperation and break down territorial boundaries. Parochialism contradicts the general direction
of reform. Of course, Shanghai should also take greater
care of other regions. As an advanced region, it should
be able to help the backward regions. Through joint ventures among enterprises, among communes, among counties,
and among provinces, the whole country can form a unified
market based on natural economic combinations. Within
this unified market, several economic centers and trade
centers can be formed. Economic activities among these

economic centers can be interconnected without any restrictions imposed by administrative boundaries.

At present, two things should be done in relation to institutional reform. First, adopt fiscal management by level. There are many problems in this area that are being studied at present. Second, expand enterprise autonomy, mainly in terms of enterprise profit retention.

At present, our concern with enterprise autonomy is not complete, but primarily in terms of profit retention. In Shanghai, several hundred enterprises in two industries (metallurgy and textile) participated in experimenting with profit retention. Much experience was gained. Many conflicts were also exposed. The most serious conflict is uneven distribution of hardship and joy among enterprises. Since we have not completed our adjustments in the national economy, some enterprises are not producing normally due to external reasons. The size of enterprise profit does not depend primarily on how well enterprises are managed and operated. Rather, it depends on prices and tax rates, etc. The products of some enterprises command high prices and large profit, while the products of other enterprises command low prices and small profit. Even among products with high prices and large profit, some (such as cigarettes and alcoholic drinks) have high taxes and small [after tax] profit, and some (such as watches) have larger profit than taxes. Even within one industry, profit varies according to types of products (such as cotton fabrics versus dacron). If the same method of profit retention is applied to all cases, it would not be fair. Many regions adopt many different methods to regulate, resulting in a very complicated system of profit retention. In the future, it is necessary to gradually adjust prices and tax rates so that profit rates among enterprises can be more even and can reflect enterprise performance. In addition, enterprises operate under different conditions. New enterprises do not need to replace machines and equipment. Old enterprises need to renew their equipment. Production funds derived from profit retention thus need to be redistributed.

Shanghai conducted an experiment within a bureau or a company. Part of the retained profit was held by the bureau or company. The rest was held by enterprises at the basic level. With this method, the company could use the profit obtained to even out the uneven distribution of hardship and joy among enterprises at the basic level and to help enterprises which needed to renew their machines and equipment. If the basic-level enterprises get too little, their activism in improving their operation and management may be adversely affected.

At present, expansion of enterprise autonomy is limited to profit retention. In fact, there are many other problems to be solved, such as management power over labor wages. At present, there are some surplus staff and workers in many enterprises for whom no alternative placements can be found. But the enterprises are again forced by labor departments to place another batch of children of staff and workers. Some plants have organized financially independent collective enterprises to open up productive opportunities with good results. But there are also plants which farm out jobs that they can do themselves to "collective enterprises," amounting to increasing their own staff and workers. With so many young job seekers waiting to be placed, it looks as if it may not be possible to quickly reform the "iron rice bowl" system of job security. To promote employees and issue bonuses according to the proportions specified from above also makes it difficult for enterprises to restructure their wage system to suit their own conditions so as to better implement the principle of distribution according to labor. Some plants suggest that they be allowed to devise their own methods of promotion and bonuses provided that they stay within the total wage bill. This suggestion is worth considering.

Enterprises should also have the autonomy to adjust their prices within limits according to state stipulations. At present, many enterprises want to increase prices. The state must exercise strict control. But with respect to many overstocked products, enterprises should have the autonomy to reduce prices within a certain limit to avoid deterioration and loss. Prices for some producer goods are obviously unreasonable. Abundant products command high prices and large profit. Scarce products command low prices and small profit. Business departments in charge and local price control departments should accept enterprises' requests to rapidly adjust prices. This can only bring benefits and no costs to the national economy and people's livelihood. It will not reduce fiscal revenues either. These requests should not have to be approved at each and every level, resulting in delay and indecision.

Reform should not be limited to expanding enterprise autonomy. It is especially important to increase the number of circulation channels. Only this way can the economy be enlivened. In the past, we had only one circulation channel--namely, state commerce. With so few circulation channels, circulation links naturally multiplied. As a result, there was a great distance between producers and users, leading to mismatch between production and needs. On the one hand, many products were often sold out. On the other hand, many products were overstocked. If socialist countries do not solve this problem, their economy will not survive. Therefore, commerce departments proposed to change the method of

unified purchase and guaranteed marketing. They favored
selective purchase and independent marketing. In the
first half of last year, commerce departments partially
adopted the system of selective purchase. Commodities
which were judged to be slow-moving were purchased at a
reduced level. Therefore, light industry was starving
for work, with a consequent drop in growth rate. In the
second half of the year, the scope of independent
marketing by industry was enlarged a little. Purchase of
commodities by the state was also increased. As a
result, industrial production picked up speed. Independent marketing should also be expanded with respect to
agricultural and sideline products. Communes and brigades should be allowed to market their own products.
Can rural communes and brigades be engaged in commerce?
Some comrades still have doubts on this point. I think
communes and brigades can participate not only in agriculture and industry, but also in commerce. It is not
speculation and manipulation for communes and brigades to
market their own products. In the past, long-distance
transportation was regarded as speculation and manipulation. This view is wrong and needs to be changed. We
cannot rely on supply and marketing cooperatives alone to
purchase all the agricultural and sideline products. It
is already difficult for them to complete their own purchase tasks. They have little time to worry about products outside their purchase plans. Communes can purchase agricultural and sideline products from production
teams and members, and sell them to supply and marketing
cooperatives or market them independently. This way
agricultural and sideline products can be better transported outside.

Last year, after farmers' markets were opened up in
various places, prices were basically stable and tending
slightly downward. Prices for some products were temporarily too high. They will come down once sales pick
up and production increases. This kind of free market
for agricultural and sideline products can become an
important supplement to state commerce. Supply and
marketing cooperatives should still be retained in towns
where farmers' markets are held to purchase and transport
agricultural and sideline native and special products.
With huge capital investment and extensive connections,
supply and marketing cooperatives will remain major
circulation channels for long-distance shipment. Like
state commerce in the urban areas, their leadership
position in the market will not be threatened.

Before adjustments in the national economy are
completed, reform should be pursued in step with adjustments. This year, due to retrenchment in capital investment, orders for the machine-building industry are
greatly reduced. Some staff and workers and machines

and equipment are idled. At the same time, for a long
time, it has been difficult for many plants to replace
and increase some machines and equipment because their
needs were not included in the allocation plan for machine products. Recently, the Center called upon old
enterprises to tap potentials, renovate, and retrofit.
Most of the products needed for these projects are not
included in the state plan. Machine-building plants
must open up more productive opportunities by accepting
these extra-plan production tasks. Shanghai hosted
order-placing conferences to produce extra-plan products
for plants of various places. Some plants even sent task
forces to service old plants. They repaired and reno-
vated various machines and equipment. These activities
seem very promising. As a result of stopping production
on some overstocked products last year, production tasks
decreased substantially for the machine-building industry
of Wuxi city, Wuxi county and their communes and brigades. But by producing extra-plan products, they still
increased the actual output value substantially. There
are many run-down and old plants in the country. If
this job is handled right, not only will the machine-
building industry be fully occupied, other industries
(particularly light industries) can also accelerate their
rate of renovating and retrofitting, leading to over-
fulfillment of this year's production plan.

To coordinate with this above-mentioned job, we must
reform the allocation system for producer goods in a big
way this year. In the past, control over producer goods
(particularly machine and steel products with their many
and complex varieties) was too restrictive. On the one
hand, allocation was far short of needs. It was very
difficult to get what one ordered, leading to an explo-
sion of purchase agents. On the other hand, large quantities of products were overstocked in warehouses,
rusting away and idling for long periods. In the past
few years, because of heavy commitments to capital construction, there were large gaps in the allocation of
material resources. Nobody was willing to surrender
overstocked products to material resource departments for
re-allocation. In the past two years, capital investment
was reduced, leading to a marked change in conditions.
Shortage of machine products was replaced by surplus.
Supply of many abundant products was freely available.
Even for scarce products, it was easier to find plants to
produce them. Therefore, we have all the conditions to
enliven the allocation system of machine products this
year by directing our attention from purchasing to
marketing. Shanghai's service companies and trade fairs
for producer goods arranged to sell off products
overstocked for years by various bureaus, companies, and
plants with good results. I think it is necessary to

establish a permanent trade center for producer goods. Industrial bureaus, companies, and large plants can station purchase and sales representatives in this center to facilitate trade. This center (and other specialized companies) will supplement the plan allocation by material resource departments.

Steel products were the scarcest in the past. Many bureaus, companies, and plants stockpiled them even when they did not need them and used them as "hard currency" to exchange with others. Now that capital investment is reduced, demand for steel products has decreased correspondingly. In effect, most steel products have become abundant. Therefore, it is possible that allocation of steel products can also be enlivened this year. Supply of abundant products can be opened up. Or they can be sent to trade fairs to be sold. This way, it is possible that a lot of overstocked steel products intended as "hard currency" will emerge from many little warehouses and flow into the large warehouses of material resource departments. In the past, even abundant products enjoyed heavy demand so that production could not be cut back. Now that people realize what are abundant products and what are scarce products, it is easier for production and allocation departments to adjust varieties and specifications, and for overstocked steel products that are widely scattered to be gathered up. Thus, it is possible to enliven the circulation channels of steel products. Of course, this is still a tentative plan. Whether it can be realized still requires a great deal of effort. If allocation of machines and steel products with their many varieties can be enlivened, allocation of coal, timber, etc. with their lesser varieties can be improved with even greater ease. We hope that great strides can be taken this year with respect to reform of the allocation system of producer goods, which has been a source of headaches for many years.

For many years, many local industries sprang up, leading to many duplications and wastes. It was like fighting a battle of attrition over an extended front. This year, it is necessary to combine or reorganize many poorly conceived small plants. Some industries should form joint ventures, or specialized companies, according to the principle of coordination through specialization, in order to upgrade production technology and management. Shanghai, Beijing, Tianjin, and other large cities have conducted some successful experiments in this respect. They should push ahead, sum up their experience, and extend it gradually. Many neighborhood plants in Shanghai increased their output several times in 20 to 30 years. Their plants cannot be expanded. It is even difficult to remodel them once they get run-down. They got organized. In addition to internal adjustments, they entered into joint ventures with commune and brigade industries. I think this is a good method, worthy of extension. Yantai of Shangdong province and Changzhou of Jiangsu province had similar experiences. As a result of combination between urban and rural areas, and between state and big collective industries on the one hand and commune and brigade industries on the other, rural areas adjacent to industrial cities have gradually industrialized and become new socialist rural areas that are both industrial and agricultural.

In short, adjustment and reform must be carried out in coordination. At present, initial success has been achieved in this respect. But many problems and conflicts still remain. They need to be seriously studied and gradually solved. To adopt plan regulation in combination with market regulation presents greater complications than just plan regulation alone. If we attempt to simplify our work, we can only give up market regulation and strangle the economy. To enliven the economy, we must introduce market regulation. But then the economy becomes more complex. We must not be afraid of difficulties. New conditions must be studied to come up with timely solutions for new problems. This is a road that must be taken for the sake of socialist modernization.

10
Comments on Reform
of the Economic System

The reforms in our economic management system carried out since the Third Plenary Session of the Party's Eleventh Central Committee in the winter of 1978 have been, I think, correct in direction, steady in pace, and substantial in results. There have been confusion and difficulties. But these are inevitable in the process of reform. In general, destruction has not been sufficient and progress is still far short of the goal. In the past year or so, we managed to make only a dent in the old system. We must advance from our victory. Since we have still not completed our task in adjusting the national economy, we can only steady our pace and introduce small reforms in preparation for big reforms this and next year.

There are three reasons, I think, for the many difficulties encountered in the reforms carried out in the past year or so. First, many comrades failed to appreciate the reforms. They still looked at new problems according to their old experience. To overcome this problem, we must conduct extensive theoretical research and publicity. Second, the few pilot projects encountered great resistance as they came into conflict with the current management system as a whole. We must gradually enlarge this breach and should not retreat from it. Third, many reforms were not coordinated. To overcome this problem, an overall plan must be made for institutional reform and reform work must be better coordinated.

The economic management system is in fact a concrete expression of the socialist public ownership system. It involves a series of theoretical and practical issues. At present, no country in the world has successfully clarified these issues. China is no exception in this.

First published in People's Daily, June 10, 1980.

Therefore, I can only raise questions today and cannot provide a concrete proposal to resolve these issues.

Last year, we tested institutional reform from two aspects. One was to use income distribution to encourage production and concern for profit while taking care of the material interests of the Center, the localities, the enterprises, and the individuals. The other was to reduce dislocations between production and needs in the area of circulation by opening a breach in the system of unified purchase, guaranteed marketing, and plan allocation and by gradually allowing the market to perform its regulating functions. Much has been achieved in these two aspects. But the national economy is a system. Various reforms inevitably interact. It is quite possible that one reform may hinder another reform. For example, reform in income distribution addresses the vertical relationship between higher and lower levels, while reform in circulation addresses the horizontal relationship between production and needs. Since interactions between the vertical and horizontal relationships were little studied in the past, contradictions between these two relationships may well arise. For instance, fiscal management by level (two-level fiscal management has developed into three-level fiscal management in many places) encourages various levels of government to be responsible for their fiscal management and should therefore be encouraged. But in a few places, a "separatist" tendency is emerging. This results in profit competition between the higher and lower levels. Furthermore, the horizontal relationship in the economy is adversely affected. If this tendency is allowed to continue, this represents a definite economic retrogression. How to consolidate the positive effects and avoid the negative effects deserves our serious study.

Second, in the past enterprise autonomy was increased primarily through profit retention. That is, enterprises were encouraged to improve operation management through income distribution. In the past year or so, this proved to be effective in most of the pilot enterprises. We should affirm this policy. But at present, product prices greatly deviate from their values. The size of enterprise profit is largely determined not by how well an enterprise is managed, but by how high prices are. Therefore, profit retention results in uneven distribution of hardship and joy among enterprises. The ultimate solution to this problem is to adjust prices. But because price adjustments are very complicated, they are not practicable at present. To reduce uneven distribution of hardship and joy, we can vary the ratio of profit retention according to the existing size of profit. However, once this method is implemented, it will become an obstacle to later price

adjustments. Every price adjustment will affect the size
of retained profit to the enterprise. If prices are set
too high, fiscal revenues are reduced. If prices are set
too low, enterprises suffer. In the end, profit is still
calculated according to the pre-adjusted prices to avoid
disputes. Not only is this method complicated to calculate and contentious, but price adjustments no longer can
regulate supply and demand. Price increases for scarce
products do not bring in higher profit to enterprises,
which therefore have no incentive to increase production.
Price reductions for abundant products do not reduce
profit to enterprises, which therefore are reluctant to
reduce output. In summary, how institutional reforms can
be effected with income distribution changes and how
dislocations between supply and demand can be avoided
through market regulation deserve serious study.

Both rights and duties should be considered in
expanding enterprise autonomy. Since profit is shared,
state investment must be compensated and interests must
be paid for quota circulating capital. In the past,
enterprises did not have to compensate the state for
investment. They naturally wanted to use as much capital
fund as possible. Machines and equipment could always be
stored for future use. If state funds are channeled
through banks as interest-bearing investment loans,
enterprises will be more careful in the use of funds.
They will economize on funds, shorten construction time,
bring in profit earlier, and reduce interest payments.
In Shanghai, six capital construction projects were to be
financed through bank loans. Two projects were volun-
tarily withdrawn after it was discovered that there was
no market for their products. At present, there are many
capital construction projects that are uncertain about
their supply of raw materials, fuels, electricity,
technology, and market. I think this is a good method to
reduce the size of capital investment. I propose that
the pilot projects in enterprise autonomy not concentrate
merely on their rights to the neglect of their duties.
The scope for compensated investment in fixed assets and
interest-bearing quota circulating capital (to reduce
inventory) should be expanded. There is little risk in
accelerating our pace in this area. Of course, production costs of enterprises will be increased and certain
adjustments in the fiscal system must be made.

Third, reforming the management system through
income distribution is not conducive to changing the economic structure. Also, it conflicts with the retrenchment of capital construction. Of the existing 300,000
plus industrial enterprises, there is a lot of duplication in production. And some industries need to be
merged according to the principle of coordination through
specialization. There are several hundred automobile

and tractor plants in the country. Together with the
coordinating plants, they number several thousands. This
is obviously too many. But they belong to several
Central ministries and many provinces and counties. To
protect their profit, they are reluctant to let the
plants go. Each plant guards its autonomy jealously and
refuses to follow orders from the parent company. The
same phenomenon arises in the silk and tobacco
industries. After fiscal affairs are managed by level,
government at all levels wants to increase its fiscal
revenues. The most common practice is to run more
plants. While the Central government wants to retrench
capital investment, the lower levels want to expand it.
In this year alone, there are about 1,000 municipalities
and counties planning to produce refrigerators, electric
fans, television sets, washing machines, and audio tape
recorders. This mad rush will inevitably result in a lot
of insolvency, thus bringing substantial loss to the
state. To gain more retained profit, all enterprises
want to "tap potentials, renovate, and retrofit." They
compete for raw materials, power supply, and market. It
is good that enthusiasm is stimulated. But the enthusiasm to build new and expand existing facilities is
already very high. Blind enthusiasm should not be
encouraged any further. This point should be carefully
kept in mind in institutional reform.
     It is definitely correct to expand local and
enterprise autonomy. And we must continue to do so. The
problem is how to consolidate the positive effects and
avoid the above-mentioned negative effects. After
repeated consideration, I conclude that the problem lies
in managing enterprises according to the administrative
system. Whether they are managed by department or by
level, it is still administrative management and not
economic management (according to objective laws of economic development). In many capitalist countries, fiscal
affairs are also managed by level. Why, then, do they
not have this problem? The reason is because their
enterprises are privately owned. The state cannot interfere with their operation. Our enterprises are publicly
owned. If they cannot be managed by one Central
ministry, they are then managed by different departments,
and by level. In fact, they are owned by the state, the
department, and the region. Because enterprise profits
are directly or indirectly delivered to the Central
Ministry of Finance, the various departments, and the
regions, all of these must interfere with the economic
activities of enterprises to increase their fiscal revenues. They must see to it that enterprises increase
profits, and they must also take a larger share of the
profits. They are not concerned with whether such

interference will destroy the organic relationships in the national economy and its proportional relationships.

To preserve the organic and proportional relationships in the national economy, it is necessary that departments and regions do not interfere with the economic activities of enterprises for their own benefits. It is necessary to devise a good method to "disengage" government agencies from enterprises, so that they only ensure adherence by enterprises to goals and policies for developing the national economy, and not interfere with concrete economic activities of enterprises. This is especially important in changing the economic structure according to the principle of coordination through specialization. During discussion, many comrades have come up with the idea to replace profit with taxes, and to gradually retire the system of delivering profit to the higher level. Instead, enterprises would pay industrial and commercial taxes, and income taxes to government at various levels. This method is used in capitalist countries. But whether it is practicable in socialist countries or not, we do not have any practical experience. Maybe we can test it out in several medium and small cities. Of course, many contradictions can also arise with the tax method. The question is which method is more conducive to managing the economy according to objective laws for economic development. We must depend primarily on plan regulation, and use market regulation under the guidance of planning. Plan management must be particularly strengthened in the adjustment period.

In the past year, I think we have achieved a lot in enlivening the national economy through reforms in the circulation channels. We reduced the scope of unified purchase and guaranteed marketing (consumer goods) and plan allocation (producer goods). We started to use market regulation to improve chronic dislocations between supply and demand. After the completion of the three great transformations, we basically have had only one circulation channel. In the urban areas, it is the commerce department. In the rural areas, it is the supply and marketing cooperative. In foreign trade, it is the Ministry of Foreign Trade. Unified purchase, guaranteed marketing, and plan allocation have erected a great wall between production and market needs. Such dislocations between supply and demand result in substantial waste for the national economy. Particularly with respect to the allocation of producer goods, many abundant products are still allocated by plan when they should be allocated freely. Plants are ordered to close down and reduce production when there are still unmet needs. Now that we admit that producer goods are also commodities and can be subject to market regulation, the situation begins to improve.

There are many hundreds of thousands of kinds of producer goods. It is obviously impossible for one agency to allocate all of them. Nor is it enough to hold 10,000-people order-placing conferences once or twice a year. Last year, many big cities convened their own order-placing conferences and held trade fairs (material exchanges) to facilitate direct contacts between producers and users. Many bureaus, companies, and enterprises were selling from their warehouses products that had been accumulated for many years, making many scarce products (such as wrapped wires) into abundant products. Because of retrenchment in capital construction and import of foreign equipment, many machine-building plants did not have enough work to do. On the other hand, many plants needed to renew their machines and equipment but could not get them from the material resources bureau because they had not been included in the state plan. Through direct contacts at order-placing conferences, producers and users solved their long-unsolved problems easily. In the past, enterprises stored everything allocated to them in their warehouses. Now, tickets are issued for some goods, which are withdrawn only when they are needed. As a result, only half of the tickets are used and inventory in the warehouses of the material resources bureau increases correspondingly. In the past year, we have found a way to reform the material resources management system. But more work needs to be done if reform is to be thorough.

The system of unified purchase and guaranteed marketing for consumer goods has also been partly changed. In the beginning of last year, the Ministry of Commerce began to selectively purchase certain consumer goods. The smaller orders forced some light industries to reduce their output. In the first quarter, output increased by only 1.4% compared with the corresponding period the previous year. Later, the Center decided to increase purchases by the Ministry of Commerce. And what was not purchased by the Ministry could be sold by the plants on their own. As a result, output in the second half of the year increased markedly and the original plan was overfulfilled. After selective purchasing and independent marketing were implemented, many plants reduced their output of abundant products and increased their output of scarce products. They also trial-marketed new products with a market demand. Dislocations between supply and demand were thus greatly reduced. In some big and medium cities, such as Shanghai, communes in their own municipalities or outside their own provinces were allowed to sell their own products in the urban areas. The result was higher income for the peasants and greater supply for the cities. At present, there are still disputes between industry and commerce regarding selective purchasing and independent marketing. Some plants marketed scarce products on their own and sold only abundant products to the commerce departments. There are still reservations in most areas about opening up markets for agricultural and sideline products in the cities. It is feared that market order may be disrupted by speculation and manipulation if communes are allowed to sell their products in the cities. To change this situation, our thinking must be liberated and more research is needed to resolve various contradictions.

Even though we have only taken some initial steps to reform the circulation channels for producer and consumer goods, the results are remarkable. In the past, with unified purchasing and guaranteed marketing, plants did not know what goods were abundant and what goods were scarce. They blindly produced according to plan. Now that this market information is available, plants need to increase output of scarce products and reduce output of abundant products. But according to current plan prices, many abundant products command high prices and large profit and many scarce products command low prices and small profit. There is a conflict between output adjustment and profit retention. To adjust output according to market needs, prices must be adjusted (with rises and falls, the general price level need not be affected). But to adjust prices, it is necessary to change the existing method of profit retention. For some products, not only must prices be adjusted, but the tax rates must also be adjusted (for example, tax for tobacco and alcoholic drinks is high and profit is small). Furthermore, resistance to price adjustments is strong, since they inevitably affect profit distribution between industry and commerce, and between the Center and the localities. But to allow this situation to continue will result in great losses to the national economy and seriously lower economic efficiency in production. Therefore, institutional reform cannot be approached on a piecemeal basis. Instead, there must be an overall plan. Each reform measure must be considered in terms of its chain reaction. Hence, it is necessary to establish a comprehensive research organ to study institutional reform so that various conflicts can be reasonably resolved.

As to future institutional reform, I think it is more important to reform the circulation system than to reform the income distribution system if the economy is to be enlivened. But this point is often overlooked by most people. To reform the circulation system, the number of circulation channels must be increased and the number of circulation links must be reduced so that producers and users can have direct contact with one another. Under the guidance of state planning, there must exist a certain degree of competition. Without this competition, the bureaucratic style of state industry and state commerce will never be overcome. With this method, state commerce is still the mainstay of a unified socialist market. But it must be supplemented with collective commerce and farmers' markets (free markets for agricultural and sideline products). We must allow commerce to combine with industry and allow production for independent marketing or for direct sale to retail stores. We must allow communes to sell their own agricultural and sideline products in the cities, or to sell to supply and marketing cooperatives. We must revive warehousing, commercial agents, exchanges, and other commercial organizations. We must revive the original business activities of banks to facilitate the turnover of funds. In short, in order to exploit the regulating functions of the market and facilitate development of our socialist economy, it is necessary to adopt certain economic institutions developed by capitalist countries for large-scale social production.

China is a big country. It is impossible to exercise a completely unified control over it. But it is also impracticable to develop 29 provinces, municipalities, and regions into 29 independent economic units. In Western Europe, nine countries saw fit to form the Common Market. In many countries, multinational corporations are being formed. These show that to divide economic activities according to administrative boundaries violates objective laws of large-scale social production. It is also not appropriate to revive the large coordination districts, because they will still be administrative districts, such as dividing up the one economic district consisting of Hebei, Shangdong, and Henan provinces into three big coordination districts. In surveys, many comrades suggested the revival of historically established economic centers. For example, Shanghai was the economic center for southeast China and connected to the whole nation. Tianjin was the economic center of north China and was connected to the northwest and the northeast. Guangzhou was the economic center of south China. Chongqing was the economic center of the southwest. Hankou and Xian were the economic centers of central and northwest China. There were no boundaries among these economic centers. They intertwined and were organized according to objective laws governing economic activities. Economic centers are mainly commercial centers, but production can also be organized. Economically advanced areas can establish jointly operated trans-provincial companies in backward areas, and use their advanced technology and capital to exploit resources in backward areas for mutual benefit. Shanghai has already started doing it.   I think there is a great future for it.   It is better than fiscal assistance, which provides only capital but not technology.   The establishment of economic centers and trans-provincial companies can perhaps break open obstacles erected by administrative boundaries.

At present, there are several dozen financial and economic departments in the State Council.   There are eight departments in the Ministry of Machine-Building Industry alone.   They are further divided into military and civilian uses.   The more detailed the specialization, the more difficult it is to coordinate them.   Each department wants to be self-sufficient and is reluctant to coordinate with other departments or localities, resulting in substantial losses.   Therefore, institutional reform must do away with vertical and regional obstacles.   In the past, the fight had already been between the dominance of vertical management and the dominance of regional management. We must think of a new way out and reform our economic structure and economic institutions according to objective economic laws governing large-scale social production.   This is a difficult problem.   We must all try to solve it.

11
Economic Structure and Reform of the Economic System

Since the Third Plenary Session of the Party's Eleventh Central Committee, we have realistically summed up the experience of 30 years of economic work, started to adjust the national economic plan and reform the economic management system, and achieved remarkable results. Admittedly, this work is difficult and complicated. It is not possible to complete it in one or two years. Many new situations and new problems arise in our work. It is necessary to liberate our thinking and rack our brains in analyzing and comparing different ideas and proposals to facilitate decision making at the Center. Below, I will talk about my personal understanding of these problems in accordance with the guidelines suggested by the Center.

I. MULTIPLE MODES OF OPERATION UNDER
   THE SOCIALIST ECONOMY

Marx and Engels' theory on scientific socialism continues to develop in practice. In the Communist Manifesto, Marx and Engels summarized their theory in one sentence: "Eliminate private property," and with it exploitation and classes. After the Paris Commune failed, Marx clearly pointed out in 1875 in his Critique of the Gotha Program that socialism was the elementary stage of communism. In this stage, some traditions or remnants of the old society must still be retained. In this book, Marx explained the principle of distribution according to labor. Because he thought that the proletarian revolution would win victory first in the most developed capitalist country, he envisioned a public ownership over the whole society. In such a society, there would no longer be commodity exchange and money could be transformed into

First published in Red Flag, 1980, No. 14.

labor coupons.   This is a great ideal.   In Marx and
Engels' time, there was no practical experience with
socialism. We should not expect them to reveal all the
details of socialism.

After the October Revolution in Russia, Lenin summed
up the positive and negative experience with war-time
socialism and the New Economic Policy, and pointed out
that commodity and money relations would still exist
for a long time in the socialist period. After he successfully guided the completion of agricultural collectivization, Stalin pointed out in his 1936 report on
constitutional issues that two kinds of socialist public
ownership still existed in the socialist society. Therefore, there would still be the working class, the peasant
class, and the educated element. This was a new development in socialist thought. Whether commodities still
existed after the ownership of means of production had
been socialistically transformed remained contentious in
Russia.   In summing up the experience of socialist construction in his later years, Stalin clearly pointed out
in Socialist Economic Problems in the Soviet Union that
as long as two kinds of socialist public ownership
existed, there would still be commodity exchange, and the
law of value would play a role. This was again another
new development in socialist thought. But he did not say
anything on whether commodity exchange would still exist
after the two public ownership systems were merged into
one ownership system for the whole society.   It still
remained a contentious issue. Comrade Mao Zedong pointed
out that commodities might still exist even after collective ownership had made the transition to whole people
ownership. Comrade Liu Shaoqi also pointed out that commodities could not be eliminated as long as distribution
according to labor could not be eliminated.

Stalin failed to appreciate the uneven regional economic development in a big country like the Soviet Union,
and thought that a single mode of whole people ownership
would suffice for the whole country without any consideration for disparities among regions and enterprises.
He also thought that a single mode of collective ownership would suffice. Moreover, important means of production (land, agricultural machines) could be owned only by
the state. And the principle of exchange of equal values
was violated in the purchase of agricultural products.
Although Stalin admitted that exchange between the two
ownership systems was still commodity exchange, he denied
that the law of value still regulated agricultural production.   Moreover, he thought that the products
exchanged among enterprises within the whole people
ownership system were actually not commodities.
Therefore, the economic management system established

under his direction emphasized only plan regulation and not market regulation.

The level of economic development in old China was even lower than that of Czarist Russia. There was extreme unevenness in economic development among regions. Several centuries separated the advanced from the backward regions. In such a country, it is all the more necessary to use historical materialism to scientifically study how socialism should be built after the proletariat has seized political power. We completed the socialist transformation of ownership of means of production in eight years. In the past, we thought it was a complete success. It now appears that we proceeded too fast during the last two years. And in some respects, we overdid it. In 1958, there was a "commmunist fever" to establish people's communes. We gradually retreated within two to three years. But we have still not completely overcome the one-sided pursuit of things big and public in our thought. We learned from the Soviet Union to have only one mode of whole people ownership and one mode of collective ownership. In the urban areas, we attempted to eliminate collective ownership. And in the rural areas, we disallowed different modes of operation to suit local conditions and attempted to prematurely eliminate remnants of individual economy. Under the guidance of this thought, China also adopted an overly centralized and unrealistic economic management system that emphasized only plan regulation and not market regulation.

Commodity economy in China's broad rural areas is still very underdeveloped. If commodity economy is not developed and if the market is not used, it is impossible to develop large-scale social production and hence to build socialism. The socialism in China's rural areas today is an immature socialism built upon a semi-natural economy. It will not do justice to confine economic construction within the communes. Economic relations between the urban and rural areas must be developed. Most of China's capitalist industry and commerce had not developed to the stage of monopoly capital. There were no various economic organizations (such as trusts) developed to expand joint economic ventures. Since the beginning of the 50's, we followed the experience of the Soviet Union by adopting the method of administrative management by department and region. Even the few original economic relations were severed. We got rid of the market economy suited to modern large-scale social production which was developed by the capitalist world for 200 to 300 years. In its place, we established another type of economy which, to some extent, restricted the development of productive forces. We must realize that

socialism is not a product of a few people's imagination.
It must be developed from a social basis. The idea that
we can skip over the development stage of a commodity
economy and eliminate overnight the inevitable disparities of the real world by establishing a "pure socialism"
does injustice to Marx's historical materialism.

To build a socialist economy in China, we must allow
many modes of operation and, to some extent, a few other
economic elements to co-exist, with socialist public
ownership occupying an absolutely dominant position.
Whole people ownership should not adopt only a single
mode. It must allow various industries, regions, and
enterprises with different degrees of mechanization and
different scales of operation to adopt different modes of
operation and management. Collective ownership has all
the more reason not to adopt a single mode. The degree
of public ownership varies in various economic units.
Within the economy under whole people ownership, there
can be some elements under collective ownership. And
within the economy under collective ownership, there can
also be some elements under individual ownership.
Collective ownership in the urban areas differs from
collective ownership in the rural areas. It is all the
more different from whole people ownership. Because of
the great disparities in economic conditions among
regions, there is all the more reason for rural collective ownership to adopt multiple modes. The principle of
"three-level ownership with the team as the basis" is
basically suited to the development level of productive
forces in most regions of the country. A few communes
and brigades have well-developed enterprises. Those communes whose incomes at the commune and brigade levels far
exceed the incomes of their production teams have already
made their transition to brigade ownership. Some of them
have made transition to commune ownership. These several
modes are mostly appropriate. On the other hand, the
production teams in a few regions of the country still
cannot guarantee minimum livelihood needs of their members. Here, in addition to encouraging the enthusiasm of
their members for the collective economy, it is also
necessary to use their enthusiasm for the individual
economy. This is particularly true for sparsely populated, mountainous, and nomadic regions. To impose by
force large-scale collective labor on these regions inevitably lowers labor efficiency and results in huge
waste. We should be even more flexible with the ownership issue. The criteria to evaluate the superiority of
ownership systems lie primarily in which can facilitate
improvement of social productive forces and labor productivity, and produce the highest economic returns. To
ask for things "big and public" apart from these criteria
is an unrealistic pipe dream.

I think there is still plenty of room for collective ownership in the urban areas, and it was a mistake to eliminate collective ownership. At present, "big collective" enterprises in the urban areas are in fact "small whole people" enterprises. Apart from the fact that a small part of the profit from collective industries goes to the Second Bureau of Light Industry for its disposal (this permitted many urban "big collective" industries to develop faster than state industries),[1] "big collective" industries are not much different from state industries in operation, management, labor compensation, etc. Since 1970, many cities have established quite a few "small collective," namely street enterprises. We did not follow completely the principles governing collective ownership in our treatment towards them. Moreover, we often elevated them to state or "big collective" enterprises without due compensation. For a long time, there seemed to be the thought that collective ownership in the urban areas was a thing of the past. Starting from last year, in order to solve the problem of labor unemployment, many cities have established financially independent cooperatives and cooperative small groups. But many people regard these as temporary measures to solve labor unemployment and labor reserves for state enterprises. Whenever state enterprises advertise for workers, members of these cooperatives all go to compete for these "iron rice bowls." Beijing is a good example of a city where urban collective ownership is better developed. But even here members of cooperatives still regard their jobs in the cooperatives as "paper rice bowls." Many people doubt the continuing existence of these collective organizations. Many cooperatives were formed with administrative fiats. The basic principles governing collective ownership such as voluntarism, financial independence, profit sharing with labor, and democratic management were not strictly adhered to. Municipal committees decided that whole people enterprises and collective enterprises should be treated equally. But some departments only half-heartedly implement this decision. Collective organizations are still treated as inferior. Under these circumstances, it is hard to consolidate under collective ownership. As to individual laborers who do not exploit others, they are faced with even greater discrimination.

Last year, in some poor rural areas, a system was adopted which assigned production responsibility to the group, or the household, or the individual in some cases, and which distributed income according to output. The increase in output was remarkable. Assigning responsibility to the household or to the individual is different from allocating land to the household. Land is still publicly owned. The production team has a unified plan and provides unified leadership. Collective labor is still retained where it is conducive to agricultural productivity.

To increase the degree of public ownership in agriculture, it is not always necessary to expand collective production. It is also possible to organize the production units within a much larger scope through supply and marketing relations. In Yugoslavia, individual peasants occupy a dominant position. But joint agricultural-industrial-commercial enterprises organize state farms, cooperative farms, and individual farms into a common body combining agriculture, industry, and commerce through supply and marketing relations. These common bodies are much larger than our people's communes. The degree of product commercialization, mechanization, and socialization is much higher than ours. It seems that to organize agricultural labor through circulation channels is also a pretty good mode of organization. Before agriculture was collectivized in China, we also organized the peasants through supply and marketing cooperatives. Of course, with so little available land for so many people in China, it was not possible for a family with 10 mu of land to mechanize its operation. It was also very difficult to level and consolidate land, and to irrigate. Therefore, it was necessary to get organized. But, agricultural collectivization must suit local conditions and adopt multiple modes of operation. Any mode of operation adopted must facilitate improvement of labor productivity and economic returns.

Last year, laws for joint enterprises between Chinese and foreign capital were announced. Thus, another new economic element will emerge. If we can allow capitalist countries to invest in China, we can certainly allow overseas Chinese and Chinese in Hong Kong and Macau to invest in China. Since last year, joint public-private enterprises of this type have started to develop in many places. Recently, the Federation of Industry and Commerce in Shanghai organized a patriotic construction company. It has raised 50 to 60 million yuan of capital to build housing for overseas Chinese and to give loans to medium and small enterprises, especially collective economic organizations. Similar companies are being formed in Tianjin and Beijing. I think the capital funds provided by these patriots, particularly their experience in operation, management, and market regulation, will be helpful to our socialist construction. The constitution allows the existence of individual laborers who do not exploit others. I think there should be some developments here in the next few years. Restauranting, tailoring, repairing, and other service activities in the urban areas are all hand labor that are suited to scattered operation. The best arrangement is to use financially independent cooperatives, cooperative groups, and individual labor. The socialist public ownership in China is already well consolidated. The existence of some semi-socialist or nonsocialist economic elements is not going to affect the dominant position of the socialist economy. Under the strong leadership of the socialist state economy, a large auxiliary collective economy and a small supplementary economy of other economic elements may well point to a way which the socialist construction of China must follow.

II. DEVELOP COMPARATIVE ADVANTAGE BY EMPHASIZING STRENGTHS AND AVOIDING WEAKNESSES

China is a big country, with more than 970 million people and 9.6 million square meters of land. We must build an independent and relatively complete economic system within the country. It was entirely correct that we proposed such a goal. But it was wrong when we tried to build a complete economy in every coordination district or even in every province or region. Natural conditions differ a great deal throughout the length and breadth of China. Each area has its own characteristics. Our goal of economic construction should emphasize strengths and avoid weaknesses so that each area can develop its comparative advantage. Coordination through specialization and exchange should be developed on a nationwide basis. Each area has its strengths and weaknesses. Shanghai is the most developed industrial region. But it lacks natural resources. Many regions in the northwest and the southwest with abundant natural resources are not developed. Coordinated specialization should be developed between these two types of regions so as to fully develop their comparative advantage for their mutual benefits.

To compete in the world market, it is necessary to develop our comparative advantage by emphasizing strengths and avoiding weaknesses. In international competition, our strengths are abundant labor power, low cost of living, and abundant resources. Our weaknesses are capital shortage, low technical know-how, and poor management. Therefore, for a long time to come, we must use our abundant resources to develop more labor intensive industries and less capital (technology) intensive industries. Only when this comparative advantage is developed can capital be gradually accumulated to permit some important industries to rank with the most advanced world standards.

In making arrangements for the domestic economy, it is all the more necessary to develop as much as possible the comparative advantage of various regions according to their natural strengths and weaknesses. In the past, every region wanted to build a complete economy. Thus, coal and iron bases were built even in regions where there was no coal or iron, resulting in great waste of manpower and capital. In agriculture, food grain was elevated to be the key crop, even in mountainous, pastoral, and subtropical regions, resulting in great destruction of local resources. In the past 30 years, we subjectively wished to rapidly reduce regional disparities. But objectively, regional disparities were not reduced. Instead, they widened. One of the reasons was the adoption of erroneous construction policy. For example, forests in mountainous regions were destroyed to create cultivated fields, and grazing pastures were destroyed to plant food grain, resulting in soil erosion, water loss, and desert expansion. Another reason was poverty manifested in low accumulation and low standard of living. In some areas, large-scale farmland capital construction was blindly pursued even when simple reproduction could not be ensured. The little manpower, material, and financial resources that they did have were thus not available for current production. As a result, people's livelihood was not improved for many years. In some cases, even the little surplus they had was squandered. In fact, the sparsely populated mountainous and pastoral regions have abundant natural resources which are sorely needed in the domestic market. Many resources are even hot items in the world market after they are processed. If the comparative advantages of these regions had been systematically developed in the past 30 years, there would not have been such shortages of raw materials in the advanced industrial regions, and light industry would have developed to a greater extent. Income of backward regions also would have greatly increased. The economic outlook would have been rapidly improved.

In general, capitalist countries developed their agriculture first, then their light industry, and finally their heavy industry. Socialist countries can shorten this process but cannot change it. Within China, advanced and backward regions must specialize. If everybody wants to be complete and self-sufficient, then no one can develop a comparative advantage. Backward regions should fully exploit their strengths by developing agriculture, livestock industry, forestry, fishery, etc. They should start with providing raw materials, and advance gradually toward rough processing and refined processing. In view of China's shortage of light industrial raw materials, backward regions should fully exploit their superior natural conditions to develop production of raw materials. This is an important way to develop comparative advantage. These regions with their

vast territories and abundant resources have strengths
unmatched by the plains. If these regions fully develop
their comparative advantage according to local conditions, the income of the people in mountains and
grazing pastures may exceed that of the people in the
plains, or even that of the workers. Several north
European countries export their timber, and Australia
exports its wool at a handsome profit. Why can't our
mountainous and grazing regions learn from their experience?

China is a socialist country. We need an overall
plan to develop regional comparative advantages, and
since there are irrationalities in our price policy and
commercial system, it is still necessary for the Center
to make overall arrangements to develop regional comparative advantages. For example, the province of
Heilongjiang exports in large quantities petroleum,
timber, coal, and food grain, which are scarce nation-
ally. With these four "trump cards," it appears that
Heilongjiang should enjoy superior comparative advantage.
But with the exception of petroleum, the other three
products command low prices and small profit. Heilongjiang often does not make any profit in exporting these
products. In some cases, it even loses money. Before we
further raise prices of timber, coal, and food grain, we
can consider setting rational internal accounting prices
and subsidizing the estimated losses through budget
appropriations. In addition, since these products cannot
be sold locally and must be sold outside the province,
the inflow of large amounts of money leads to regional
demand inflation. When the state formulates the commodity circulation plan, it should plan to ship in an
appropriate amount of light industrial products according
to the principle of exchange of equal values. Otherwise,
the comparative advantage of Heilongjiang cannot be developed. Take another example. Cow hide, wool, meat,
milk, etc. from Inner Mongolia are all scarce products.
At present, income of herdsmen in Inner Mongolia's
pastoral regions is markedly above that of peasants in
the food grain regions. As a result, the comparative
advantage of pastoral regions has been partly developed.
But after exporting large quantities of pastoral products, they still cannot buy their daily commodities.
Here again, commerce departments must also supply daily
commodities according to the principle of exchange of
equal values to ensure an affluent life.

To develop regional comparative advantages, we must
as far as possible gradually increase prices for agricultural, pastoral, forest, and fish products, and other
raw or processed materials. We should also gradually
change the system of unidirectional plan allocation, and
approximately equate inflows to outflows. At present, we

should consider allowing raw material producing regions
to exchange products exceeding plan requirements for what
they need from other provinces at "negotiated prices"
after they have fulfilled their allocation assignments.
Or they can be allowed to ship these raw materials to
other provinces for processing on a profit-sharing basis.
Product allocation between urban and rural areas should
also follow similar principles to encourage production in
agriculture, livestock industry, forestry, fishery, and
other raw materials. If we thoroughly implement these
principles, not only will regional comparative advantages
be encouraged, regional disparities will also be reduced.

III. PROTECT COMPETITION, PROMOTE JOINT VENTURES

     During the three-year recovery period and the First
Five-Year Plan period in China, there was acute competition between the state economy and the private economy.
At the time, the state economy was very strong and easily
defeated the capitalist economy. After socialist transformation was completed, the state economy became a
monopoly. Because of centralized control and responsibility and lack of competition, bureaucratism in management grew stronger day by day. Our economic structure
and economic activities gradually became rigid. After
the Third Plenary Session of the Party's Eleventh Central
Committee, reform of the economic management system was
started. Plan regulation was combined with market regulation. Market functions were fully exploited under the
direction of plan. In the past year or so, we began to
open a breach in the system of unified purchase and
guaranteed marketing (consumer goods) and plan allocation
(producer goods). For many daily commodities, output was
set according to sales. Commerce departments purchased
selectively. And what was not purchased could be sold by
plants on their own. Conferences to place orders,
exhibit, and sell products were convened in center cities
for some producer goods. For products not included in
the allocation plan, extra-plan exchange was carried
out. In the past, agricultural and sideline products
were monopolized by supply and marketing cooperatives.
Commerce departments were not allowed to go down to the
rural areas, and supply and marketing cooperatives were
not allowed to go to the urban areas. Exchange between
urban and rural areas was hindered. Now the boundaries
between urban and rural areas are beginning to be broken.
In some regions, communes and brigades are allowed to
ship their products to urban areas for sale. Although
the amount of products marketed independently by plants,
communes, and brigades is not large, some competition in
the market begins to emerge. Also, because producers and

users can have direct contacts, it is easy to tell what products move fast and what products move slowly. This forces production departments to adjust their production plans, and commerce departments to adjust their purchase and marketing plans. Dislocations between production and needs begin to improve. Some plants begin to send people out to market their products, study user needs, or advertise to attract customers. Because of this competition, some shops run by commerce departments improve their service to customers. At present, these new conditions are just starting to emerge. If we could only let them develop naturally, the results would be more marked day by day.

To adopt market regulation, we must allow competition and protect competition. Since free market is a capitalist principle, we have shied away from talking about competition. We only accept emulation. Competition and emulation are not entirely the same. In competition, because the winning enterprises can earn more profit and winning staff and workers can receive more bonuses, there is a drive to improve production technology, operation, and management. Of course, socialist competition is different in principle from capitalist competition. Our competition is based on public ownership of means of production and guided by the state plan. It is not free competition. Competition must be combined with material incentives. Otherwise the advanced cannot be rewarded and the backward cannot be disciplined. For many years, because we objected to combining material incentives with competition, enterprises were treated equally whether they made or lost money. And staff and workers were treated equally whether they worked hard or not. This impeded improvement in production techniques, and in operation and management. Furthermore, it led to dislocations between production and market needs, neglect of economic returns, and great waste. Some comrades were afraid of competition for fear of widening disparities. In fact, it is exactly this kind of disparities that rewards the advanced and disciplines the backward. Disparities objectively exist, and cannot be rapidly eliminated by subjective measures. Today we admit disparities in order to rapidly develop production and create favorable conditions for eliminating disparities. Egalitarianism reflecting the viewpoint of petty bourgeoisie is not scientific socialism.

Protecting competition not only meets with ideological resistance, it also conflicts with our current rules and institutions. Our current rules and institutions permit every industry to monopolize, and every region to be autonomous without interference from one another. Competition is almost always restricted, if not totally banned. Therefore, in order to protect competition, it

is necessary to reform current rules and institutions
which impede competition, and break down separatist
blockades among industries and regions. Protecting competition may also lead to conflict with the local interests of some regions and departments. In the past more
than 20 years, we called upon various regions to
establish complete industrial systems and build a lot of
"five small industries."*2 Most of the output from these
"five small industries" is of low quality, high cost, and
high resource consumption. It will inevitably be eliminated in competition. In some areas, the government
forbids purchases or orders from advanced units outside
their own areas in order to protect these backward enterprises. Obviously, these interferences from local
governments ultimately impede development of their own
enterprises.

Protecting competiton also conflicts with the
current system of price control. Prices are an important
tool in competition. To allow only one set of prices in
the whole national market is not conducive to competition
among regions and enterprises (including companies). At
present, all enterprises must follow the unified plan
prices. Prices of fast-moving products are not allowed
to be raised and prices of slow-moving products are not
allowed to be reduced. Enterprises are not allowed to
set higher prices for good quality and low prices for
poor quality. Many products with inferior quality and
high cost are supported with sales quotas or fiscal subsidies. High-quality and low-cost products are often
prevented from competing in the market because of restrictions from unified purchase and guaranteed marketing
and plan prices. To protect competition, price departments should give enterprises a certain degree of autonomy to set prices. Plants with low cost due to advanced
technology and good management should be allowed to sell
more at a lower profit margin. High-quality products
using scarce raw materials should be allowed to command
higher prices so that they can fully exercise their competitive power.

In the past two years, we gradually corrected the
international closed door policy set by Lin Biao and the
"Gang Of Four" and boldly entered the world market.
Quite obviously, our products must be competitive if they
are to be successful in the world market. Before they
are to compete in the international market, they must
first compete in the domestic market. It is not possible
to win in the Olympic Games if there are no sports meets
at home. To protect competition, we must oppose economic
blockades imposed by any region, and forbid administrative measures to exclude entry of products from other
regions into local markets in order to protect their

backward industries. There should be regional specialization so that one region's weaknesses can be compensated
by other regions' strengths and one region's strengths
can compensate other regions' weaknesses. In the past,
enterprises were forbidden to operate across industries
and regions. This should be changed. The former is not
conducive to comprehensive utilization of resources, and
the latter is not conducive to organizing product
exchange according to economic channels. Enterprises
from different industries can be integrated (such as
integration between coal mines and electricity generating
stations). Purchasing and marketing agencies can be
established among regions after consultation. The monopoly held by commerce departments and supply and marketing
cooperatives in domestic trade, and by the Ministry of
Foreign Trade in foreign trade, should be gradually
relaxed. At present, there is an urgent need to increase
circulation channels, and permit competition. Without
these changes, "bureaucratic commerce" can never be
contained.

Capitalist countries treat free competition as the
motive force for economic development. It is used to
encourage enterprises to continually raise their technical level, and improve operation and management so that
their products can meet the needs of the market and win
in competition. After monopoly organizations were widely
developed, many countries passed "anti-monopoly laws" to
protect medium and small industries and ensure that free
competition can still serve as the motive force to a certain extent. This is a necessary measure to prevent economic atrophy. In the European Common Market, there is
free trade among its members by lowering tariff barriers.
This is an inevitable result of a highly developed social
economy. We should learn from this experience. Of
course, since ours is a relatively underdeveloped
socialist economy, it is still necessary to continue
the policy of external control to protect our economic
autonomy. (It is best not to let the Ministry of Foreign
Trade monopolize this control. Instead, the Ministry
should organize relevant industries and regions into
joint operations).

The result of protecting competition is to force
industries and enterprises to reform or reorganize in
order to avoid elimination. Won't a lot of medium and
small enterprises be forced into bankruptcy as a result
of this policy? This can be avoided by encouraging
mergers. At present, there are a few enterprises which
lack resources, waste energy, and produce low-quality,
high-cost products. These enterprises cannot be transformed. They must be allowed to stop production or be
merged with advanced enterprises. Most of the medium and
small enterprises can exist independently. Some of them

can enter into joint ventures with large enterprises. In capitalist countries, coordination through specialization results in large plants organizing small plants to produce parts for them. Many small plants are also willing to coordinate with large plants to ensure steady production. Since ours is a socialist country, coordination through specialization among large and small enterprises should be easier to organize than in capitalist countries if it is properly guided. And the phenomenon of "big fish swallowing little fish" can be completely avoided. In the past, many large and small plants found it difficult to arrange for coordinated specialization. The main reason was that some of our plants belonged to several central ministries, some belonged to provinces, municipalities, and counties, and some were "big collectives" and "small collectives." All were managed according to administrative convenience and not according to economic laws. After joint corporations were formed, the member enterprises were still under the control of their respective governing administrative organs. There was no unified control in the joint corporations. If we reform our economic management system so that they can get away from these unreasonable interferences from the administrative management organs, these joint ventures are completely realizable.

With the rapid development of local, commune, and brigade industries, there are conflicts between producers of agricultural raw materials and manufacturing plants. Communes want to process products left over from fulfilling their delivery quotas themselves (such as tobacco leaves, silk cocoons, etc.). They even sell the inferior products to the state and keep the good products for themselves. The result is that output of high-quality products in manufacturing plants is reduced, adversely affecting export and domestic trade. The British-American Tobacco Company of old China integrated the cigarette rolling plants in Shanghai and Qingdao with the tobacco producing areas in Xuchang of Henan, Fangzi of Shangdong, and Fengyang of Anhui, etc. It produces brand-name cigarettes according to fixed recipes. At present, cigarettes and tobacco are controlled by the light industry bureaus and supply and marketing cooperatives of several municipalities and counties. The tobacco producing areas have their own small cigarette rolling plants producing low-quality cigarettes. Because of a shortage in raw materials, output of brand-name cigarettes in Shanghai and Qingdao is decreasing day by day. This trend completely violates the direction towards large-scale social production. Under present circumstances, the effective way to resolve this conflict is to encourage joint ventures (coordination). In addition to organizing joint corporations, communes and brigades should be allowed to share profit by delivering raw materials in excess of output quotas to state enterprises. In the past, many regions established small chemical fertilizer plants and small iron and steel plants to gain access to chemical fertilizers and iron and steel, resulting in substantial losses. In the future, they should be encouraged to invest in large plants. In addition to profit sharing, they should be given some chemical fertilizers and iron and steel. With this arrangement, localities will not be tempted any more to establish small plants which produce low-quality products with high cost and high consumption of coal and electricity. With the institution of fiscal responsibility and enterprise profit retention, localities and enterprises have more capital funds at their disposal. If leadership is not provided, it is possible that duplication in capital construction in excess of market needs may occur, resulting in competition for raw materials, coal, electricity, and market, and substantial loss to the state economy. Therefore, we should encourage joint operations between the Center and the localities, and among provinces, municipalities, counties, big collectives, and small collectives under the planned guidance of the state. Such joint operations can rationally allocate the capital funds of localities, enterprises, communes, and brigades by breaking down industrial, regional, and ownership boundaries and avoiding blind duplication in capital construction. Joint operations are a matter of direction at present.

There are now 300,000 industrial enterprises under whole people ownership and more than one million enterprises under collective ownership. Some of these must be reorganized according to the principle of voluntarism and mutual benefit. The method is to organize them into joint operations according to the principle of voluntarism and mutual benefit. They are entitled to profit and product sharing according to a certain ratio. In Shanghai, there are many neighborhood plants which have increased their output by several tens of times in the past 30 years and are unable to expand their plant facilities. Now, in addition to merger and reorganization within the municipalities, they also go outside the municipality to establish joint operation with commune and brigade plants. They contract out certain simple operations to commune and brigade plants. They use the latter's land, plants, and labor and assist them with technicians and management personnel. This way, production can still continue. But urban congestion can be reduced and rural industry can be developed, with the prospect of gradually developing into a socialist countryside which combines agriculture with industry. Beijing, Tianjin, and other places also have successful experience with joint operations and organizing companies as a means to reform the industrial economic structure.

Joint enterprises should assume many forms, such as joint investment, cooperative operation, processing of supplied materials, and compensation trade. They could be in the form of companies or joint ventures according to economic needs. Companies that are established by leadership organs from above through administrative fiats usually violate the principle of voluntarism, mutual benefit, and management by economic means, and are therefore not viable. At present, since we lack experience, joint enterprises should proceed from the bottom to the top, from the small to the big, and from the simple to the complex. At first, some loosely integrated units should be started. Steady advance is then built upon that basis. Some industries (such as the machine-building industry) are suited to organizing companies for coordinated specialization. Some industries (such as textile industries) are suited to independent plant operation, with the company coordinating the relation among plants and serving them. Plants that are organized into coordinated specialization within a company must still be financially independent. They must also be allowed to enter into business relations with other enterprises outside the company, provided that they have fulfilled their coordination contracts first. In joint corporations with independent enterprises (such as textile companies), it is also possible to set up a common fund from part of the enterprise profit under an overall arrangement within the industry. This fund can be used to help some plants in technical renovation, or to help plants with obsolete machines to install new equipment. There is no need for many industries using mainly manual labor (such as food, tailoring, and home furniture) to be organized into companies. They can be operated on a scattered basis. At present, there is both a tendency to concentrate and a tendency to scatter in capitalist countries. The number of independently operated small plants and small shops is quite large. It is not necessary to organize all industries and may lead to unnecessary waste if it is carried out.

IV.   ESTABLISH ECONOMIC CENTERS, DEVELOP
       TRANS-PROVINCIAL COMPANIES

Apart from resolving the vertical relations between the top and the bottom, reform of the economic management system can more importantly resolve the horizontal relations between production and needs. To do this, it is necessary to fully utilize market functions under plan guidance, transform our economic organization according to product circulation needs, and establish trans-industrial and trans-regional economic relations. In the course of historical evolution of the commodity economy, a large number of large, medium, and small cities have sprung up to serve as centers for economic linkages. The original economic centers were formed gradually in the process of economic development. They met the objective needs of economic development. After socialist transformation of capitalist industry and commerce was completed, we destroyed the original economic channels and gradually replaced economic centers with administrative centers. If economic relations between Shanghai and south Jiangsu must be realized through Nanjing, and economic relations between Shanghai and Liaodong Peninsula must be realized through Shenyang, the number of procedures and costs must increase, resulting in substantial loss of time and economic efficiency. After the goal of combining plan regulation with market regulation was announced in the Third Plenary Session of the Party's Eleventh Central Committee, some big cities began to serve as economic centers. For example, Shanghai trial-hosted a national order-placing conference mainly for producer goods patterned after the "Canton Trade Fair." Companies and enterprises from all over the country could send representatives to sign supply and marketing contracts. Direct contacts between producers and users began to solve the long-standing problem of concentrated ordering twice a year. That this old practice did not meet the needs of plants could be seen by the large number of active purchasing agents.

Shanghai has also hosted a trade fair for producer goods (now known as display and sales fair). Bureaus, companies, and enterprises from various regions could list their overstocked products in catalogs or advertise them on wall posters to attract buyers in the fair. Bureaus, companies, and enterprises who needed these products did not need to go through a lengthy application procedure with the material resources bureau, nor did they need to send purchasing agents all over before they could meet their needs. Instead, they could easily buy what they needed right there at the fair. In the past, material resources bureaus were unable to supply many scarce products. In fact, there were scattered stocks in various warehouses. When they were pooled, there were enough to meet needs. For many years, bureaus, companies, and enterprises always applied for more material resources than they needed. These surpluses were often accumulated for 10 to 20 years. Through the trade fair, they saw the light once more and could be put to good use. In the past, producer goods were stuck once they arrived at their destination. Now through the trade fair, they came alive again. Similar organizations have been set up in Beijing, Tianjin, and other large cities. Of course, it is just starting now. In the future, trade fair buildings need to be constructed in which bureaus, companies, and large enterprises of various regions can set up offices to conduct trade on a regular basis. Beijing plans to set up an "international trade center." Why can't we build several "domestic trade centers"?

In the past, there were many economic centers in the country. Shanghai was the economic center in southeast China and was connected to the whole country. Tianjin was the economic center in north China and connected to the northwest and northeast. Guangzhou was the economic center of south China and connected to the southwest. Shenyang was the economic center of the northeast, Wuhan was the economic center of central China, Chongqing was the economic center of the southwest, and Xian was the economic center of the northwest. Under these economic centers, there were also many, many smaller economic centers. According to the regional characteristics of various economic centers, they could also serve as distribution centers for several major products. These economic centers were naturally formed according to objective conditions (production, transportation conditions, etc.). Unlike artificial administrative boundaries, they were more adaptable and flexible. Since these economic centers already exist, they need only to be used, not started from scratch. As to how we can use them, we should refer to historical experience on the one hand, and adapt them to suit the socialist system and the economic development of the past 30 years on the other. Once this direction is pointed out, the concrete methods can be left to regional ingenuity.

Regions must not only expand the number of circulation channels but also integrate production. Shanghai has already formed more than ten trans-provincial companies to integrate with plants in other provinces. The results have been good. Shanghai is China's biggest industrial base. It has great potentials in terms of capital, equipment, and manpower. But its own industrial development has already reached a saturation point. Therefore, the future direction of Shanghai's industrial development is on the one hand to develop sophisticated products and let other regions produce the less sophisticated products, and on the other hand to reach outward to set up trans-provincial companies. It can also develop foreign markets. Shanghai lacks raw materials. It can establish raw material producing bases in other provinces. Last year, Shanghai jointly operated five paper-making plants with other places, in this way basically satisfying Shanghai's need for paper for writing, printing, and packaging. Shanghai lacks timber. It can invest in joint ventures with mountainous regions in the northeast and southwest to process timber. It lacks leather. It can invest in joint ventures with places in the northwest and Inner Mongolia to process leather. At present, Tianjin, Beijing, and other cities are also preparing to invest in trans-provincial companies. This move is beneficial to both the advanced and the backward regions. In the past, budget appropriations to aid backward regions could not solve the problem of technical know-how. Trans-regional integration may produce much better results. We even welcome investment from capitalist countries. We should all the more welcome investment from advanced areas and backward areas in the country.

Will the establishment of economic centers and the development of trans-provincial companies widen economic disparities between advanced and backward regions? There may be a temporary tendency in this direction. In the long run, this is the only way to reduce regional disparities. The United States of America was first developed from 13 states. After more than 100 years of development towards the south and the west, with enterprises in advanced areas competing to invest in backward areas, various regions in that country have all managed to develop to a very high level. At present, disparities in the level of economic development between advanced and backward areas in China are still very large. In the past, various regions could invest only within their own boundaries and were not allowed to invest outside. This was not conducive to reducing regional disparities. If we do not use the strengths of advanced areas by encouraging them to invest in the development of backward areas, but instead force backward areas to be self-sufficient or to rely on aid from the Center for capital construction, then it will be much more difficult to reduce regional disparities. Of course, economic cooperation among regions must follow principles of voluntarism and mutual benefit. Advanced areas have the duty to help backward areas. At present, investment from advanced areas to backward areas consists primarily in helping backward areas to produce and rough-process raw materials. It is designed to satisfy the urgent needs of advanced areas for raw materials and semi-processed products, and not for more profit. At the same time, backward areas enjoy the benefit of using capital and know-how from advanced areas to develop and utilize their own abundant natural resources and fully develop their comparative advantages. Even after the national economy is extensively developed, there will still be regional specialization. Since international division of labor will exist forever, regional division of labor will also exist forever within China.

Establishing economic centers and trans-provincial companies may be an effective means to build circulation and production relations among regions, to break down departmental separation and regional blockades, and to transform administrative management into economic management. This arrangement allows enterprises of various regions and industries to free themselves of departmental and regional restrictions and to combine according to natural needs of economic development. At present, there is still strong resistance against institutional reform. This results from conflicts between existing rules and institutions and pilot projects under the new management system. Our pilot projects opened up some breaches in existing rules and institutions. We must seriously sum up our experience and systematically enlarge these breaches, gradually leading to fundamental reform of existing rules and institutions. At present, Central economic management organs are much too large, with far too many departments. Interferences with economic activities from Party and government organs at various levels are also excessive. Consequently, it is difficult for enterprises (including companies) to manage economic affairs according to objective economic laws, especially according to requirements for large-scale social production. Therefore, while reforming the economic management system, it is necessary to reform our administrative management system. Administrative management organs should be simplified. And the irrational phenomenon of replacing the government with the Party should be changed. The Party should emphasize adherence to lines, goals, and policies. And the government should serve the economy (such as municipal construction, welfare, culture, education, etc.) and not usurp the economy.

EDITOR'S NOTES

*1.   China's cooperative plants were under the jurisdiction of the Second Bureau of Light Industry. While state plants had to deliver all their profit to the state, cooperative plants handed in about 50% to the state and the remainder to the Second Bureau of Light Industry for technical improvement in these plants and the establishment of new cooperative plants. See Xue Muqiao, China's Socialist Economy (Beijing, China: Foreign Languages Press, 1981), p. 41.
*2.   The five small industries are: (1) iron and steel plants, (2) coal mines, (3) machine-building, (4) fertilizer and chemical plants, and (5) hydroelectric stations.

APPENDIX A:
Contents of
Current Economic Problems in China
(Chinese Edition)

*Selections for this English edition.

APPENDIX B:
Dates of
Frequently Mentioned Events

1949–1952	Three-year recovery period
1953–1957	First Five-Year Plan
1958–1962	Second Five-Year Plan
1958–1960	Great Leap Forward
1961–1965	Five-Year Adjustment
1966–1970	Third Five-Year Plan
1966–1976	Cultural Revolution
1971–1975	Fourth Five-Year Plan
December 1978	Third Plenary Session of the Party's Eleventh Central Committee

APPENDIX C:
Conversion Table
for Units of Measurement

Chi = 14.1 inches

Jin = 1.102 pounds

Mu = 1/6 acre

Yuan = 0.57 U.S. dollar as of October 7, 1981

Index